The first major anthology of poems whose subject is entirely horses, this collection by Olwen Way covers the whole spectrum of poetry. From the classical Greek and Roman writers to contemporary poets still making their name; from the rigorous sonnet form to the flexibility of the modern; from the rollicking sporting ballad to the subtle and gentle ode; from China to South Africa, from Australia to Scandinavia, every aspect of the poet's celebration of the horse is represented.

In nearly 300 poems and extracts, the horse itself is also explored in detail. Its birth, its activities under saddle and between the shafts, its old age and death are all focal points. Different characters, both horses and horsemen, fill the pages, creating every mood from fun to satire to pathos. The beauty and nobility of the horse and its great achievements over history are enhanced by the poetic structures in which they are described.

Here there is something for everyone who loves poetry and who loves horses. A special feature of the anthology is that not only can it be dipped into, in common with other collections, but that it is arranged in such a way that it can be read from beginning to end, like a story or an adventure, as each poem is linked in subject, atmosphere or thought with the one which follows. Part of the pleasure of reading the poems in this way is in the satisfying associations between poems and the feeling of completeness which this gives the anthology as a whole.

With illustrations specially drawn for the poems, this book will be picked up again and again, to renew old acquaintances, to make new friends, and to satisfy all moods. Through its pages the poetry lover will come to know horses and the horse lover will come to know poetry.

THE
POETRY
OF
HORSES

~

When all the light and life are sped
Of flowing tails and manes,
And flashing stars, and forelocks spread,
And foam-flecks on the reins;

I like to think from every land
And far beyond the wave
A crowd of ghosts will come and stand
In grief around that grave —

FROM *The Mourners*
WILL H. OGILVIE

THE
POETRY
OF
HORSES

~

A COLLECTION BY
Olwen Way

ILLUSTRATED BY
Belinda Sillars

J. A. Allen
London

British Library Cataloguing in Publication Data
A catalogue record for this book is available from
the British Library

ISBN 0.85131.611.5

Published in Great Britain in 1994 by
J. A. Allen & Company Limited
1 Lower Grosvenor Place
London SW1W 0EL

Designed by Nancy Lawrence

Phototypeset by Wilmaset Ltd, Wirral
Printed by Dah Hua Printing Press Co. Ltd.,
Hong Kong

DEDICATION

To all thirteen of my grand-children in the hopes that one day
their love for horses and ponies may be equalled by their love
for poetry!
James, Kate, David, Lucy, Victoria, Jessica, Sophie, Fay,
Lydia, Abigail, Ben, Charlotte and Jonathan.

CONTENTS

~

ACKNOWLEDGEMENTS

~

My thanks go to my son, Gregory Way, for the free run of his excellent library.

To my friend Penny Radclyffe for her unfailing support and enthusiasm.

To my cousin, Professor David McMullen, for helping me find the lovely Chinese poems.

To Alison Brackenbury for allowing me to use any of her superb poems from a generous collection.

To Elizabeth O'Beirne-Ranelagh of J. A. Allen without whose help and encouragement this book would never have arrived.

Olwen Way

INTRODUCTION

Poetry is subjective writing. It is concerned with the writer's feelings and emotions; it is his imaginative response to his subject. Selecting poetry for a collection such as this is also subjective.

There are two aspects of this anthology which set it apart from other collections. The first is that, although it can be dipped into for favourite poems and authors using the contents list or the indexes at the back of the book, it has a structure of its own. I have tried to structure it in such a way that it can be read from beginning to end as a sort of adventure, taking us through not only the life of a horse but also the different styles and eras of poetry.

The second difference is that it includes several previously unpublished poems and authors. The poems by Peter Cornish and Penny Radclyffe, among others, are presented here for the first time, as are Richard King's beautifully crafted translations of a number of Chinese poems. The translator feels that in order to increase the reader's understanding and enjoyment of these poems it is important to realise the force of their allegorical nature, and the tendency of the poets to identify themselves with the horses they describe: steeds of unlimited potential needing only a wise master to recognise their talents.

In the structure of the book, each poem is linked by some kind of association with the one which follows it. It is a subjective connection, somewhat like a 'train of thought'. For instance, we have started with the mare about to foal, and foals and young horses are explored in the following poems. Una

Auld's 'Handling the Colt' ends on the theme of friendship, which is picked up by Will H. Ogilvie's 'A Comrade'. His 'charger on parade' turns into 'Military Governor Wei's Red Charger' in the next poem, and here the link of 'the greatest wish of every boy' is further explored in Raine Maria Rilke's poem, 'The Boy', who wants to 'drive with wild black horses through the night'. There follows a section on horses from mythology, which gallop across the sky to bring night or day, drawing chariots or bearing warriors. This brings us through two or three links to poems on the young and ponies suitable for them.

The next section, on parting, buying and selling, and loyalty, leads on to horses in battle, which meld into horses from the sea, and another section on mythical and historical ideas. Fantasy, dreams and unreality follow on, and in the same vein David Campbell's 'The Stockman' considers the idea of time, which leads us into modernisation and the horse versus the car and the tractor. A natural link here is the cart horse and his various functions, and two poems on cart-horse stallions lead us into a general section on stallions, stabled horses and horses at pasture.

Philip Larkin's 'At Grass' forms the link between this and one of the longest sections, which covers the past glories of all sorts of horses, from 'The High-Mettled Racer' to 'The Little Worn-Out Pony'. Some have received kind treatment, but others have not been so lucky. The achievements of racehorses such as 'Red Rum' and 'Brown Jack' brings us into a section on racing which carries into galloping, the idea of the chase, spectacular leaps, and so into hunting and its controversies. We come home from hunting and other rides to a brief evening by the fire in Will H. Ogilvie's 'Storm-Stayed', before going out again to ride through snow and storms, in all weathers.

A series of linked poems covering many different subjects follows. We explore romance, death and superstition; the 'white-Lyard' horse of one poem becomes 'A Roan Horse' in the next, and the longing for spring in this poem makes some horsemen think of shows! Various types of pony lead into celebrations of specific horses, such as Alison Brackenbury's 'Five Horses'. This section ranges from ordinary working horses to the most highly bred. Descriptions of their action and conformation, a sort of 'verbal sculpture', span the centuries: there are no chronological or national boundaries for the portrayal of beauty. This is also true of the next section on horsemanship.

Finally, the brave horsemen who fought in times past lead into the last section on death of both horses and people. We complete the circle with our final poem, which brings us back to the beginning with the foaling mare.

The intensely personal relationship between horse and human is often romantic and lyrical, as well as explicit and poignant; for example, the defection of Richard II's horse serves to highlight the pathos of his master's situation as perceived by Shakespeare.

So many poems, so many horses. I hope that the reader will find my choice pleasing, and I can only reiterate the words of Will Ogilvie which preface this book.

VERNON WATKINS
The Mare

~

The mare lies down in the grass where the nest of the
      skylark is hidden.
Her eyes drink the delicate horizon moving behind the
      song.
Deep sink the skies, a well of voices. Her sleep is the
      vessel of Summer.
That climbing music requires the hidden music at rest.

Her body is utterly given to the light, surrendered in
      perfect abandon
To the heaven above her shadow, still as her first-born
      day.
Softly the wind runs over her. Circling the meadow, her
      hooves
Rest in a race of daisies, halted where butterflies stand.

Do not pass her too close. It is easy to break the circle
And lose that indolent fullness rounded under the ray
Falling on light-eared grasses your footstep must not yet
      wake.
It is easy to darken the sun of her unborn foal at play.

~

ANONYMOUS
The Horse Breeder's Prayer

~

St George,
Thou saintly chevalier,
With all my heart I implore thee
To mares and stallions thou art dear –
Secure one favour for me!

See here!
My blood congeals with fright;
The pedigree grand mare is foaling.
Give her the best of foals tonight
And send my cares a-rolling!

~

[3]

FERENC JUHÁSZ
Birth of the Foal

TRANSLATED BY
David Wevill

~

As May was opening the rosebuds,
elder and lilac beginning to bloom,
it was time for the mare to foal.
She'd rest herself, or hobble lazily

after the boy who sang as he led her
to pasture, wading through the meadowflowers.
They wandered back at dusk, bone-tired,
the moon perched on a blue shoulder of sky.

Then the mare lay down,
sweating and trembling, on her straw in the stable.
The drowsy, heavy-bellied cows
surrounded her, waiting, watching, snuffing.

Later, when even the hay slept
and the shaft of the Plough pointed south,
the foal was born. Hours the mare
spent licking the foal with its glue-blind eyes.

And the foal slept at her side,
a heap of feathers ripped from a bed.
Straw never spread as soft as this.
Milk or snow never slept like a foal.

Dawn bounced up in a bright red hat,
waved at the world and skipped away.
Up staggered the foal,
its hooves were jelly-knots of foam.

Then day sniffed with its blue nose
through the open stable window, and found them –
the foal nuzzling its mother,
velvet fumbling for her milk.

Then all the trees were talking at once,
chickens scrabbled in the yard,
like golden flowers
envy withered the last stars.

~

[4]

WILL H. OGILVIE

FROM

The Old Mare's Foal

~

'*She* was the best that I ever had,
   She needed no whip nor spur,
Game as a pebble, and this game lad
   Is the living image of her –
Same old courage and jaunty tread,
   Just like the good old soul!
I could pick him out of a hundred head,
   In the dark, as the old mare's foal.'

~

FRANK KENDON

FROM

The Time Piece

~

With lifted heads, with level backs, tails flying
Three foals in paddock show their grace and breeding,
Their young hooves doggedly thudding the closecropt turf
Hither come thundering, stepping forth from delight,
Over the pond-side knoll, round by the pyramid holly,
Up to the top of the slope, far off, where the fence begins.
There, to a sudden standstill fetch'd, they front the wind,
Wild as the wind and proud in poise by nature,
And whinny above brisk wilderness of reeds
To the distant hissing hushing and narrow sea.

And the patient mares stand dreaming by the water.
Till one, the dark one – loosening her strong neck,
Drops her skull, lips the faultless mirror,
And draws a steady, cool, sustaining drench;
Thence raising lazily that dripping muzzle again,
Workless and wise, the noble careworn head
Rejoins a doze she scarcely interrupted.

And ringlets on the glassy water widen away from her
Flagging softly among the weeds and diamond dragonflies.

~

[6]
VERNON WATKINS
Foal
~

Darkness is not dark, nor sunlight the light of the sun
But a double journey of insistent silver hooves.
Light wakes in the foal's blind eyes as lightning
          illuminates corn
With a rustle of fine-eared grass, where a starling shivers.

And whoever watches a foal sees two images,
Delicate, circling, born, the spirit with blind eyes leaping
And the left spirit, vanished, yet here, the vessel of ages
Clay-cold, blue, laid low by her great wide belly the hill.   ·

See him break that circle, stooping to drink, to suck
His mother, vaulted with a beautiful hero's back
Arched under the singing mane,
Shaped to her shining, pricked into awareness
By the swinging dug, amazed by the movement of suns;
His blue fellow has run again down into grass,

And he slips from that mother to the boundless horizons of air,
Looking for that other, the foal no longer there.

But perhaps
In the darkness under the tufted thyme and downtrodden winds,
In the darkness under the violet's roots, in the darkness of
       the pitcher's music,
In the uttermost darkness of a vase
There is still the print of fingers, the shadow of waters.
And under the dry, curled parchment of the soil there is
       always a little foal
Asleep.

So the whole morning he runs here, fulfilling the track
Of so many suns; vanishing the mole's way, moving
Into mole's mysteries under the zodiac,
Racing, stopping in the circle. Startled he stands
Dazzled, where darkness is green, where the sunlight is
       black,
While his mother, grazing, is moving away
From the lagging star of those stars, the unrisen wonder
In the path of the dead, fallen from the sun in her hooves,
And eluding the dead hands, begging him to play.

≈

[7]

THOMAS KYD
A Colt
≈

A fine little smooth horse colt
Should move a man as much as does a son.

≈

[8]

GEORGE ROSTREVOR HAMILTON
The Cantering Foal
~

O antics lovely to see of the cantering foal!
What human child,
    Though warm his impulse, wild his feet
    Could win so joyous, transitory, fleet,
Complete a moment, free from memory's dear burden?

Awkward and lovely the unlearnt throw of his limbs;
For me, entranced,
    The happy, momentary sight
    Shall pierce – ah, many a day! – with new delight
A musing mind, never free from memory's dear burden.

~

[9]

ROBERT FROST
The Runaway
~

Once when the snow of the year was beginning to fall,
We stopped by a mountain pasture to say, 'Whose colt?'
A little Morgan had one forefoot on the wall,
The other curled at his breast. He dipped his head
And snorted at us. And then he had to bolt.
We heard the miniature thunder where he fled,
And we saw him, or thought we saw him, dim and grey,
Like a shadow against the curtain of falling flakes.

'I think the little fellow's afraid of the snow.
He isn't winter-broken. It isn't play
With the little fellow at all. He's running away.
I doubt if even his mother could tell him, "Sakes,
It's only weather." He'd think she didn't know!
Where is his mother? He can't be out alone.'
And now he comes again with clatter of stone,
And mounts the wall again with whited eyes
And all his tail that isn't hair up straight.
He shudders his coat as if to throw off flies.
'Whoever it is that leaves him out so late,
When other creatures have gone to stall and bin,
Ought to be told to come and take him in.'

~

UNA AULD

Handling the Colt

~

Wild thing, bright thing,
Swift thing, light thing,
With the silky black hair falling over your eyes;
Nervous, excited,
Distrustful, affrighted,
Nostrils extended like twin butterflies,
Crimson and quivering,
While you stand shivering,
Shaking the silky black hair from your eyes.

Quietly – let me near!
Nothing for you to fear!
Ah! Now you're learning we're friends and not foes.
Feel me caressing,
Never distressing,
Rubbing the velvet just over your nose.
Now on the skin that's known
Wind and sun's touch alone
Gently my fingers move, steady and slow.

Sniffle . . . Don't shake away!
Closer . . . Don't break away!
Dance on your slender legs, then quiet . . . so!
Letting me nearer steal,
Nearer . . . until I feel
All that distrust like a dark dream is past.
Wild thing and bright thing,
Swift thing and light thing –
Ah! Nuzzle into me, friends, friends, at last.

~

[11]

WILL H. OGILVIE
A Comrade

(1916)

~

You only know him groomed and combed
   And bridled on parade;
I know the paddocks where he roamed,
   I saw him roped and made.

I saw him on a Queensland plain
   Unbranded and unthrown,
With mud upon his tangled mane
   And forelock backward blown.

I saw him in the breaker's yard
  Bereft of half his pride,
The foam upon his shoulder starred,
  The sweat upon his side.

He loved the wide-fenced fields, and I,
  Who loved those fields as dear,
Lived with him where the long plains lie
  Six hundred leagues from here.

You only know him groomed and combed,
  A charger on parade;
I know the paddocks where he roamed
  Ere he was roped and made.

~

[12]

TS'EN TS'AN
Military Governor Wei's Red Charger

TRANSLATED BY
Richard King

~

A painting could not do justice to your red charger;
Swift as a whirlwind, the colour of peach-blossom,
Red halter, purple reins and a whip of coral,
A jade saddle on an embroidered cloth, and a golden
    bridle.

I asked you to come out with your falconer's glove, to see
     you ride.
His tail was long and touched the ground, like red silk.
You boasted that of all horses none was his equal
Still remembering the hundred gold pieces with which
     you bought him.

In the perfumed streets and Purple Alley at the capital,
Of all the city people who saw you, none was not envious.
Stung by the whip to a flying gallop, the white sweat flowed,
He flashed past proudly with a clatter of green jade hoofs.

A barbarian with red whiskers had a golden knife and
     scissors,
He brought the scissors out at night, to give the horse a
     three-pronged mane.
When I looked in the stable, he was in high spirits
He stood out from the mass with his exceptional splendour.

The horseman has gone hunting at the foot of the
     southern mountain
South of the city, foxes and hares no longer exist.
With a light touch on the grass, so swift he seems to fly,
He looks up at the green falcon which flies but loses ground.

I remember seeing you in the early morning
Jade pendants jingling, the road filled with perfume.
I realised then how rich and noble the border-generals are,
How fine it is, when horses and men bring glory to each
     other!

The greatest wish of every boy is to be like this:
The swift horse gives a long whinny, the North Wind rises
     up,
Waiting for you to go East to sweep away the foreign
     rabble,
He would go a thousand li a day for you.

~

RAINER MARIA RILKE
The Boy

TRANSLATED BY
J. B. Leishman

~

I'd like, above all, to be one of those
Who drive with wild black horses through the night,
Torches like hair uplifted in affright
When the great wind of their wild hunting blows.
I'd like to stand in front as in a boat,
Tall, like a long floating flag unrolled.
And dark, but with a helmet made of gold,
Restlessly flashing. And behind to ride
Ten other looming figures side by side,
With helmets all unstable like my own,
Now clear like glass, now old and blank like stone.
And one to stand by me and blow us space
With the brass trumpet that can blaze and blare,
Blowing a black solitude through which we tear
Like dreams that speed too fast to leave a trace.
Houses behind us fall upon their knees,
Alleys cringe crookedly before our train,
Squares break in flight: we summon and we seize:
We ride, and our great horses rush like rain.

~

[14]

BARRY CORNWALL

FROM

The Rape of Proserpine

A verse about Pluto's four coal black steeds of the Underworld.

~

Mark him as he moves along,
Drawn by horses black and strong,
Such as may belong to Night
Ere she takes her morning flight.

~

[15]

THOMAS CAMPBELL

FROM

Pleasures of Hope

~

He comes! dread Brama shakes the sunless sky
With murmuring wrath, and thunders from on high,
Heaven's fiery horse, beneath his warrior form,
Paws the light clouds, and gallops on the storm!

~

HOMER

FROM

The Iliad xvi.181

Xanthos and Balios were the horses of Achilles.

~

The winged coursers harness'd to the car;
Xanthos and Balios of immortal breed,
Sprung from the wind, and like the wind in speed.
Whom the wing'd harpy, swift Podarge, bore,
By Zephyr pregnant on the breezy shore.

~

PERCY BYSSHE SHELLEY

FROM

Homer's Hymn to the Moon
~

And having yoked to her immortal car
The beam-invested steeds, whose necks on high
Curve back, she drives to a remoter sky
A western Crescent, borne impetuously.

Homer's Hymn to the Sun

~

. . . The immortal Sun,
Who borne by heavenly steeds his race doth run
Unconquerably, illuming the abodes
Of mortal men and the eternal Gods.
. . .

His rapid steeds soon bear him to the West,
Where their steep flight his hands divine arrest,
And the fleet car with yoke of gold, which he
Sends from bright heaven beneath the shadowy sea.

~

[18]

OVID

FROM

Metaphysics ii

An account of Phaeton driving his father's horses after a promise
fulfilled. His father was Helios – the Sun.

~

At once from Life and from the Chariot driv'n,
Th' ambitious Boy fell thunder-struck from Heav'n.
The Horses started with a sudden Bound,
And flung the Reins and Chariot to the Ground:
The studded Harness from their Necks they broke,
Here fell a Wheel, and here a Silver Spoke,
Here were the Beam and Axle torn away;

And scatter'd o'er the Earth the shining Fragments lay,
The breathless Phaeton with flaming Hair,
Shot from the Chariot like a falling Star,
That in a Summer's Ev'ning from the Top
Of Heav'n drops down, or seems at least to drop;

. . .

~

[19]

THE RIGVEDA
Hymn to the Sun

TRANSLATED BY
R. T. Griffith

In Hindu tradition, the Chariot of the Sun God is drawn by eight
horses.

~

Look! his horses mounted high,
   Good of limb, and stout and strong,
In the forehead of the sky
   Run their course the heavens along.
Praises to his steeds be given
Racing o'er the road of heaven.

Such the majesty and power,
   Such the glory of the sun;
When he sets at evening hour,
   The worker leaves his task undone.
His steeds are loosed, and over all
Spreadeth Night her gloomy pall.

~

ANONYMOUS
Saying of the Claddagh Gipsies of Galway
~

Gipsy gold does not chink and glitter.
It gleams in the sun and neighs in the dark.

~

ANONYMOUS

FROM

Vafthrudnismal

TRANSLATED BY
W. Taylor

The Scandinavian Goddess Nott (the Night) is drawn in a dark
chariot by Hrim-faxi (Frost Mane) – a black horse. Rime drops
from his mane and his bit. This verse is from the Eddaic poetry of
twelfth-century Iceland.

~

Hrim-faxi is the sable steed,
From the east who brings the night,
Fraught with the showering joys of love;
As he champs the foamy bit,
Drops of dew are scattered round
To adorn the vales of earth.

~

[22]

HENRY WADSWORTH LONGFELLOW
Pegasus in Pound
~

Once into a quiet village,
  Without haste and without heed,
In the golden prime of morning,
  Strayed the poet's winged steed.

It was autumn, and incessant
  Piped the quails from shocks and sheaves,
And, like living coals, the apples
  Burned among the withering leaves.

Loud the clamorous bell was ringing
  From its belfry gaunt and grim;
'Twas the daily call to labour,
  Not a triumph meant for him.

Not the less he saw the landscape,
  In its gleaming vapour veiled;
Not the less he breathed the odours
  That the dying leaves exhaled.

Thus, upon the village common,
    By the schoolboys he was found;
And the wise men, in their wisdom,
    Put him straightway into pound.

Then the sombre village crier,
    Ringing loud his brazen bell,
Wandered down the street proclaiming
    There was an estray to sell.

And the curious country people,
    Rich and poor, and young and old,
Came in haste to see this wondrous
    Winged steed, with mane of gold.

Thus the day passed, and the evening
    Fell, with vapours cold and dim;
But it brought no food nor shelter,
    Brought no straw nor stall, for him.

Patiently, and still expectant,
    Looked he through the wooden bars,
Saw the moon rise o'er the landscape,
    Saw the tranquil, patient stars;

Till at length the bell at midnight
    Sounded from its dark abode,
And, from out a neighbouring farmyard,
    Loud the cock Alectryon crowed.

Then, with nostrils wide distended,
    Breaking from his iron chain,
And, unfolding far his pinions,
    To those stars he soared again.

On the morrow, when the village
    Woke to all its toil and care,
Lo! the strange steed had departed.
    And they knew not when nor where.

But they found, upon the greensward
　　Where his struggling hoofs had trod,
Pure and bright, a fountain flowing
　　From the hoof-marks in the sod.

From that hour, the fount unfailing,
　　Gladdens the whole region round,
Strengthening all who drink its waters,
　　While it soothes them with its sound.

~

[23]

ALISON BRACKENBURY
Breaking Out
~

Pinto is out again! He kicks his door
Till the bolts give. Last time he only wandered
To the trough to gulp the freezing water
Then back into his stall. But now he bursts
Bristling to the cold, bright black and white
Through all of us, across the radiant yard.
The stablegirls run shouting. Ros
Has found the camera – Ros is young and shy,
Like a thin tree: her teeth caught in a brace,
Pale hair bunched down her spine; and all she loves
Is horses. 'I must catch him – ' Not with hands;
She has her own horse: chestnut, fine-boned, staring
As a magpie head sweeps past his door.
Feet clatter ice – it's not her own she wants –
Pinto is out! The boy sent to pile snow

Across their road, warning of six foot drifts
In the next hollow, looks up – hurls a spade
As Pinto wheels, straight through the open gate
Across the unwalked white which was the field.

The stable girl falls stumbling in a drift
But Pinto's prints, triumphant, leave a curve
As planes track a clear sky: and the sky lifts
Great, blue, unshadowed. Knee-deep in the drifts
He canters, skips, snow-shod. A while, he stops,
Scuffing his nose white, sniffing. Ros and I
Press against the wire in ice-blue shadow.
'Take him now!' I say. 'Too near,' she wails.
He plunges out of focus. He comes near
To eye my brandished carrots, meant for Glen,
Nearer, nearer. I do not want him caught.
I feel her shoulders tense, squinting at each
White step: a photograph, a means: the end
The strange eyes shining, always, out of reach.

~

D. H. LAWRENCE
The White Horse
~

The youth walks up to the white horse, to put its halter on
and the horse looks at him in silence.
They are so silent, they are in another world.

~

ROBIN IVY
Child Rider
~

He hasn't got any legs;
That is, he hasn't got

Any legs that work:
He was made that way.

He has to be dragged along
Like a rag doll. (Glad Rag Doll)

He is thin and pale
With storm-black eyes,

Living in a world
That does not speak.

Sometimes he screams.
Is it in protest?

Or is it some primordial force
Unknown to us that tears him?

Billy remains calm,
Lending him legs,

Sharing dumbness;
Raising him up

To look at trees and clouds.
Child rider looks about him,

Silent now,
At the far horizon,

Almost smiles,
Until he tires, droops,

Withdraws to see the sun go down
And he not there.

There's no more time for play,
His hands drop from the reins.

Billy stands patient and unmoving
As he slides from his saddle.

Embraced by waiting arms.
Rag doll (Sad Rag Doll)

Is taken back to his chest
And riding is over for the day.

WILLIAM WORDSWORTH

FROM

The Idiot Boy

Johnny is sent off on a pony to fetch the doctor for a sick
neighbour. The pony is described as follows.

~

. . . Mild and good,
Whether he be in joy or pain,
Feeding at will along the lane,
Or bringing faggots from the wood.

. . .

His steed and he right well agree;
For of this Pony there's a rumour,
That, should he lose his eyes and ears,
And should he live a thousand years,
He never will be out of humour.

But then he is a horse that thinks!
And when he thinks, his pace is slack;
Now, though he knows poor Johnny well,
Yet, for his life, he cannot tell
What he has got upon his back.

~

PATRICK HORE-RUTHVEN
When First a Mother Bore You

Written at the age of 8 to his favourite pony.

~

When first a mother bore you
You knew that I was for you,
You knew I did adore you,
Dolly Grey.
You knew not how you knew it
Your eyes could not see through it,
But you knew it, aye, you knew it,
Dolly Grey.

So when we both are dead and meet on further shore
We'll start together fresh,
My Dolly Grey.
We'll go roving, roving, roving, as we ever did before,
Unencumbered by the flesh,
My Dolly Grey.

~

WILL H. OGILVIE
The Gymkhana King
~

Look at the gallant old flea-bitten grey
   Lined with the others to enter the game;

Sleepy, and twenty years old if a day;
  Lean – you could hang up your hat on his frame!
But when he sees a potato and pail,
  Waiting wheelbarrow or musical stall,
Keen and aquiver from ears to his tail
  Seagull is ready to tackle them all!

Hauled on his haunches, or going full swing
  To the side of a lady with needle and thread,
Tipping the bucket or tilting the ring,
  Saddled, unsaddled, or ridden or led,
Be it a scramble, or be it a race,
  Gretna Green flight or 'Victoria Cross',
Whether it's cunning or whether it's pace
  Seagull will never be found at a loss.

Round the close poles he can bend with the best;
  Hurdles he takes with a confident stride;
Carries a gallant in finery dressed;
  Carries his lady-love sitting beside;
Stops at the tiniest touch on the rein,
  Leaps at the lightest of hints from a heel,
Swings round and races hot-footed to gain
  Place in a stall when they're playing 'John Peel'.

Many a stouter may start for a Cup,
  Many a handsomer bid for your glance,
Faster there may be when colours are up,
  Fencers there may be could lead him a dance;
But when the watchers are crowding the ropes
  Round the green fields that are flagged for the fray
Seagull's the hero to carry our hopes –
  Seagull, the gallant old flea-bitten grey!

≈

HARRY MORANT

FROM

The Nights at Rocky Bar

~

That big timber took some dodging, but our hacks were
      tried and true,
And whilst their heads were let alone, would mostly get us
      through;
Though never a horse, save Harlequin, at night, 'twas my
      belief,
Could race among those bilbee holes and yet not come to
      grief!

Those nights the brumbies tried to break straight back the
      way they came
Proved Harlequin as nimble as we knew him to be game –
In those rushing frantic scrambles 'twas his cleverness I
      thank
That I never got a smasher down that rotten, basalt bank!

And then we'd jog away to camp – two miles below 'the
      bar',
Where we'd find a pipe of 'nail-rod', and a nobbler in the
      jar!
Ah, though our lines of life since then have lain in diverse
      ways –
We don't forget those gallops of the brumby-running
      days!

~

[30]

RUDYARD KIPLING

FROM

Ballad of the King's Jest

~

And the talk slid north, and the talk slid south,
With the sliding puffs from the hookah-mouth.
Four things greater than all things are, –
Women and Horses and Power and War.

~

[31]

JACK HURLBURT

The Ridge

Written in memory of my saddle partners who have crossed over.

~

So long, old partner, 'til we meet again.
　　You stepped up and rode away.
I watched as slowly up the rock trail
　　you carefully picked your way.
Upon the ridge you rested, then turned
　　and waved one last goodbye,
You then reined west and off the ridge you dropped
　　and rode down the other side.

I'll think of you when stars grow dim
　　and red-gold comes the dawn,
Or when the evening shadows purple
　　and the night is coming on,

Or when the sky is dark with clouds
   and fresh the scent of summer rain,
For you will come a-helping when
   the big herds gather once again.

Down the steep slope you slowly go
   to the deep valley far below,
Then rest in the cottonwood's shade
   in the land of the Indian and the buffalo.
Onward down the dim trail between towering
   red walls beneath the blue sky
To where the canyon opens in to new range
   and grasses grow to stirrup high.

For here the grass is always fresh and green,
   no searing drouth winds blow,
Nor do the cattle hump and drift before
   frigid blast and blinding snow.
Then along the rocky stream you ride where
   the water runs cold and clear,
And then a greeting echoes through the valley.
'Get down, my friend, you are welcome here.'

~

[32]

WILL H. OGILVIE
The Remount Train

(1915)

~

Every head across the bar,
Every blaze and snip and star,

Every nervous twitching ear,
Every soft eye filled with fear,
Seeks a friend and seems to say:
'Whither now, and where away?'
Seeks a friend and seems to ask:
'Where the goal and what the task?'

Wave the green flag! Let them go! –
Only horses? Yes, I know;
But my heart goes down the line
With them, and their grief is mine –
There goes honour, there goes faith,
Down the way of dule and death,
Hidden in the cloud that clings
To the battle-wrath of kings!

There goes timid childlike trust
To the burden and the dust!
Highborn courage, princely grace
To the peril it must face!
There go stoutness, strength, and speed
To be spent where none shall heed,
And great hearts to face their fate
In the clash of human hate!

Wave the flag, and let them go! –
Hats off to that wistful row
Of lean heads of brown and bay,
Black and chestnut, roan and grey!
Here's good luck in lands afar –
Snow-white streak, and blaze, and star!
May you find in those far lands
Kindly hearts and horsemen's hands!

~

EDRIC ROBERTS
Four-Year-Old
~

The hammer has fallen, the auctioneer nods
    To one who becomes your new owner today.
From now is your fate in the lap of the gods,
    And we, who had bred you, turn sadly away.

For you were our care from the day you were foaled,
    A quaint little creature, so leggy and shy,
To grow, like your dam, most courageous and bold;
    And now, all too soon, we must bid you good-bye.

Perhaps, when they take you out hunting again,
    The first time you ever saw hounds will come back,
That day when we jogged to the Meet, in the rain,
    And you pricked up your ears when you sighted the pack.

Then, while we were waiting outside the oak copse,
    You shook with excitement on hearing the horn;
I could feel your heart thumping against my old tops,
    And I knew that a ready-made hunter was born.

How kindly you took to the game from the start;
    How quick to excel in each lesson begun;
So great was your courage, so large was your heart,
    You richly deserved all the plaudits you won.

But school-days are over – they fly for us all –
    And Life must be faced with its joy and regret;
To part with you, now, is our wormwood and gall,
    But we too, alas, have our living to get.

The pick of our stable, we say it with truth,
    Without you the future looks dismal and black.

Ah! Will you remember the days of your youth,
   When leading the field with some fashionable pack?

~

[34]

A. M. HARBORD

The Property of an Officer Who is Going Abroad
~

'Fifty – and five – sixty; at sixty,
Sixty I'm bid; sixty-one, sixty-two,
Sixty-two; are you done? Sixty-two,
Sixty-two' (the last moment you own him).
'Are all done? I'm bid sixty-two.
The last time!' And – rap! 'Sixty-two!'
And you turn, sick at heart, as he trots to his stall,
Just to bid him farewell and go home, and – that's all.

You bought him – remember? One day in September,
Dog-poor and leg-weary and galled angry red,
He called to your heart with his pluck and his gallantry,
Captured your soul with the cock of his head.
And the pride that he carried, mixed up in a fair;
And you couldn't go easily, leaving him there.
So you bought him and nursed him. He needed no
      schooling!
He knew it and loved it; you knew by the fooling
He played when the season came round and you tried
      him;
Remember that day? What a glory to ride him!

Your youth and his knowledge, his courage, his power
(The best gifts to Man are the Horse and the Hour);
You trusted – he gave, and was glad in the giving;
And the world was a playground, and Life was worth
      living.

It's India for you and a dealer for him,
And the yard as you leave it is damnably dim.

~

[35]

ELEANOR FARJEON

I Must Sell My Horse

~

I must sell my horse because the skies are snowing,
Nothing in the cupboard, children crying on the floor.
Never was another horse like him for going;
I must sell my horse to keep the wolf from the door.
Friend, old friend, the children want their meat,
   In another stable you'll have corn to eat.

Once he drew the rake that set the green hay flying,
Once he drew the cart that carried in the yellow corn,
Once I rode my horse because a man was dying,
Once I rode my horse because a child was born.
Friend, old friend, the children want their meat,
   In another stable you'll have corn to eat.

~

G. A. FOTHERGILL

'Bonnington' – a Four-Year-Old Chesnut

To a friend in need of a good mount

~

Sired by a hackney (the sire of three Queens),
     Foal of a mare of the Waler breed;
Petted and fed by a girl in her teens;
     Schooled in the ways of a sportsman's creed –
     This is the pony for you in your need.

All's well that ends well on straw and on sward:
     Time *was* when I found some Australian tricks –
Tricks of the race of a station abroad,
     Bucking and sidling and fore and aft kicks; –
     I soon knocked 'em out with the aid of my sticks.

Gifted with spirit – the pluck of his dam;
     Made of the tendon and bone of his sire;
Playful as kitten and kind as a lamb,
     Good-looking withal – what more d'ye require?
     Tell me at once that I have you a buyer.

Peering through bridle as straight as an arrow,
     Six mile an hour he can amble and walk,
Passing the traffic as cool as a sparrow;
     Pricks up his ears whenever I talk
     (I talk to 'em always no matter what balk.)

~

CAROLINE NORTON

FROM

The Arab's Farewell to His Steed

~

My beautiful! my beautiful! that standest meekly by,
With thy proudly arched and glossy neck, and dark and
      fiery eye.
Fret not to roam the desert now, with all thy winged
      speed;
I may not mount on thee again – thou'rt sold, my Arab
      steed.

Fret not with that impatient hoof – snuff not the breezy
      wind –
The farther that thou fliest now, so far am I behind;
The stranger hath the bridle-rein – thy master hath his
      gold –
Fleet-limbed and beautiful, farewell; thou'rt sold, my
      steed, thou'rt sold.

. . .

They tempted me, my beautiful! – for hunger's power is
      strong –
They tempted me, my beautiful! – but I have loved too
      long.
Who said that I had given thee up? Who said that thou
      wast sold?
'Tis false – 'tis false, my Arab steed! I fling them back
      their gold!

~

ALISON BRACKENBURY
Horse-Dealing
~

I am wondering whether to buy you:
you are much too strong for me
snort up the heavy ploughland
mud-splashed, a dragon, slide
to smoking halt; dance sideways out on cliffs –
undaunted, still survive
while eating more than any horse
I ever knew; can rip bare gorse
from brushwood fences. Yet the sense
I hold of you, is something else:
checked on the cold hill-path, you gaze ahead
your speckled ears sharp to catch the space
of tiny woods; crouched hills, your nose
cream as the brimmed meal-bins, lifts pale
to the great winter light. Through which I race
to someone too, in love with distances
who is – no more than you – for sale.

~

G. J. WHYTE-MELVILLE

The Clipper that Stands in the Stall at the Top

~

Go strip him, lad! Now, sir, I think you'll declare
   Such a picture you never set eyes on before;
He was bought in at Tatt's for three hundred, I swear,
   And he's worth all the money to look at, and more;
For the pick of the basket, the show of the shop,
Is the Clipper that stands in the stall at the top.

In the records of racing I read their career,
   There were none of the sort but could gallop and stay;

At Newmarket his sire was the best of his year,
    And the Yorkshiremen boast of his dam to this day;
But never a likelier foal did she drop
Than this Clipper that stands in the stall at the top.

A head like a snake, and a skin like a mouse,
    An eye like a woman, bright, gentle, and brown,
With loins and a back that would carry a house,
    And quarters to lift him smack over a town!
What's a leap to the rest, is to him but a hop,
This Clipper that stands in the stall at the top.

When the country is deepest, I give you my word
    'Tis a pride and a pleasure to put him along;
O'er fallow and pasture he sweeps like a bird,
    And there's nothing too wide, nor too high, nor too strong;
For the ploughs cannot choke, nor the fences can crop,
This Clipper that stands in the stall at the top.

Last Monday we ran for an hour in the Vale,
    Not a bullfinch was trimmed, of a gap not a sign!
All the ditches were double, each fence had a rail,
    And the farmers had locked every gate in the line;
So I gave him the office, and over them – Pop!
Went the Clipper that stands in the stall at the top.

I'd a lead of them all when we came to the brook,
    A big one – a bumper – and up to your chin;
As he threw it behind him, I turned for a look,
    There were eight of us had it, and seven got in!
Then he shook his lean head when he heard them go plop!
This Clipper that stands in the stall at the top.

Ere we got to the finish, I counted but few,
    And never a coat without dirt, but my own;
To the good horse I rode all the credit was due,
    When the others were tiring, he scarcely was blown;
For the best of the pace is unable to stop
The Clipper that stands in the stall at the top.

You may put on his clothes; every sportsman, they say,
　　In his lifetime has one that outrivals the rest,
So the pearl of *my* casket I've shown you today,
　　The gentlest, the gamest – the boldest, the best;
And I never will part, by a sale or a swop,
With my Clipper that stands in the stall at the top.

～

[40]

A. B. PATERSON

FROM

In the Stable

～

What! You don't like him; Well, maybe – we all have our
　　　　fancies, of course;
Brumby to look at you reckon? Well, no; he's a
　　　　thoroughbred horse;
Sired by a son of old Panic – look at his ears and his
　　　　head –
Lop-eared and Roman-nosed, ain't he? – well, that's how
　　　　the Panics are bred.
Gluttonous, ugly and lazy, rough as a tip-cart to ride,
Yet if you offered a sovereign apiece for the hairs on his
　　　　hide
That wouldn't buy him, nor twice that; while I've a
　　　　pound to the good,
This here old stager stays by me and lives like a
　　　　thoroughbred should:
Hunt him away from his bedding, and sit yourself down
　　　　by the wall
Till you hear how the old fellow saved me from Gilbert,
　　　　O'Maley and Hall.

. . .

So I gathered the youngster together, and gripped at his
     ribs with my knees.

. . .

But the half-broken colt was a racehorse! He lay down to
     work with a will,
Flashed through the scrub like a clean-skin – by Heavens
     we *flew* down the hill!
Over a twenty-foot gully he swept with the spring of a
     deer
And they fired as we jumped, but they missed me – a
     bullet sang close to my ear –

. . .

Yes! There's the mark of the bullet – he's got it inside of
     him yet
Mixed up somehow with his victuals, but bless you he
     don't seem to fret!

~

TU FU

Written Beside a Wall-painting of Horses by Wei Yen

TRANSLATED BY
Richard King

~

Mr Wei is leaving me, he has come to say goodbye;
Knowing how I admire his matchless painting
He playfully picks up an old brush and dashes off a Hua-liu,
Suddenly I see a Ch'i-lin coming out of the Eastern wall.
One is chewing grass, another is neighing,
I sit and see a thousand miles to the frost on their feet.
In these troubled times, where can such fine horses be
        found
That would live and die for their masters?

~

WILL H. OGILVIE

Loyal Heart

From Scotland Ogilvie wrote in his later years: 'I have ridden
many hundreds of horses in Australia, America and over here
hunting and in the Remount Department in the Great War, but
there was never a horse like Loyal Heart . . . I begin to think that
when I am dead they will find 7PD engraven on my heart.'

～

In journeys far extending,
    When courage played its part,
And sunset saw the ending
    As dawn had seen the start,
No horse the bushmen bridled could live with Loyal
            Heart.

And so that each beholder
    His worth might understand
He carried on his shoulder
    The famous **P.D.** brand
That tells us how they bred them out there in cattle-land.
. . .

I loved that grey horse madly,
    He was my boast and pride,
And Ah! but I walked sadly
    The day that Loyal died;
And when he lived no longer I cared no more to ride.

～

HARRY MORANT

FROM

Who's Riding Old Harlequin Now?

~

There was buckjumping blood in the brown gelding's
    veins,
But, lean-headed, with iron-like pins,
Of Pyrrhus and Panic he'd plentiful strains,
All their virtues, and some of their sins.
'Twas pity, some said, that so shapely a colt
Fate should with such temper endow;
He would kick and would strike, he would buck and
    would bolt –
Ah! who's riding brown Harlequin now?

A demon to handle! a devil to ride!
Small wonder the surcingle burst;
You'd have thought that he'd buck himself out of his hide
On the morning we saddled him first.
I can mind how he cow-kicked the spur on my boot,
And though that's long ago, still I vow
If they're wheeling a piker no new-chum galoot
Is a-riding old Harlequin now!

I remember the boss – how he chuckled and laughed
When they yarded the brown colt for me;
'He'll be steady enough when we finish the graft
And have cleaned up the scrubs of Glen Leigh!'
I am wondering today if the brown horse yet live,
For the fellow who broke him, I trow,
A long lease of soul ease would willingly give
To be riding brown Harlequin now!

. . .

From starlight to starlight – all day in between
The foam-flakes might fly from his bit,
And whatever the pace of the day's work had been,
The brown gelding was eager and fit.
On the packhorse's back they are fixing a load
Where the path climbs the hill's gloomy brow;
They are mustering bullocks to send on the road,
But – who's riding old Harlequin now?

~

[44]

WILLIAM SHAKESPEARE

FROM

King Richard II
Act V, Scene V

Richard gives audience to the Groom after his deposition and the
crowning of Bolingbroke as Henry IV.

~

Groom. Hail, royal prince!
K. Rich.   Thanks, noble peer;
The cheapest of us is ten groats too dear.
What art thou? and how comest thou hither,
Where no man never comes but that sad dog
That brings me food to make misfortune live?
Groom. I was a poor groom of thy stable, king,
When thou wert king; who, travelling towards York,
With much ado at length have gotten leave
To look upon my sometimes royal master's face.
O, how it yearn'd my heart when I beheld
In London streets, that coronation-day,
When Bolingbroke rode on roan Barbary,

That horse that thou so often hast bestrid,
That horse that I so carefully have dress'd!
K. Rich. Rode he on Barbary? Tell me, gentle friend,
How went he under him?
Groom. So proudly as if he disdain'd the ground.
K. Rich. So proud that Bolingbroke was on his back!
That jade hath eat bread from my royal hand;
This hand hath made him proud with clapping him.
Would he not stumble? Would he not fall down,
Since pride must have a fall, and break the neck
Of that proud man that did usurp his back?
Forgiveness, horse! why do I rail on thee,
Since thou, created to be awed by man,
Wast born to bear? I was not made a horse;
And yet I bear a burden like an ass,
Spurr'd, gall'd and tired by jauncing Bolingbroke.

~

[45]

SIR WALTER SCOTT

FROM

The Lady of the Lake
Canto Fifth

~

'Stand, Bayard, stand!' – the steed obeyed,
With arching neck and bending head,
And glancing eye and quivering ear,
As if he loved his lord to hear.

~

MATTHEW ARNOLD

FROM

Balder Dead
'Journey to the Dead'

~

But when the Gods were to the forest gone,
Hermod led Sleipner from Valhalla forth
And saddled him; before that, Sleipner brook'd
No meaner hand than Odin's on his mane,
On his broad back no lesser rider bore;
Yet docile now he stood at Hermod's side,
Arching his neck, and glad to be bestrode,
Knowing the God they went to seek, how dear.
But Hermod mounted him, and sadly fared
In silence up the dark untravell'd road
. . .
So on the bridge that damsel blocked the way,
And question'd Hermod as he came, and said:
'Who art thou on thy black and fiery horse
Under whose hoofs the bridge o'er Giall's stream
Rumbles and shakes? . . .'
. . .
Thence on he journey'd o'er the fields of ice
Still north, until he met a stretching wall
Barring his way, and in the wall a grate.
Then he dismounted, and drew tight the girths,
On the smooth ice, of Sleipner, Odin's horse,
And made him leap the grate, and came within.

~

TU FU

A Dark Piebald Horse

TRANSLATED BY
Richard King

The poet's introduction: the Emperor gave a horse to Chancellor President Lord Liang. Duke Li T'eng coveted it and got hold of it, and asked me to write a poem about it.

~

Everyone knows about Duke T'eng's feeling for horses;
So as soon as someone had a dappled piebald of the
       Ta-yuan breed
Of which he had only heard before, he decided to take a
       look.
When it was led out, all bystanders were quite astonished.

How magnificent it was, with its powerful form and easy
       movement!
Looking back at its shadow it neighed proudly, flaunting
       its prowess.
Its glowering eyes flashed darkly, as though mirrors hung
       there,
The muscles under its mane rippled, the 'joined-cash'
       markings quivered.

Next morning he tried it out briefly in his decorated chariot,
He never felt that a thousand taels would be too much to
       pay.
When tiny drops of red sweat appeared on the snow-white
       hide,
The silver saddle was taken off and replaced with a
       perfumed cloth.

When Lord Liang's horse had grown older, the Duke
       managed to get it

Second only to the very dragons in their Heavenly
        Stables.
For its morning bath, it may dive into the depths of Ching
        and Wei,
After its evening gallop, it can be groomed in the darkness
        of Yu and Ping.

I have heard that a fine thoroughbred only reaches its
        prime with age,
So in a few years this horse will astound us still more.
Why should its four hoofs, that carry it swifter than the
        birds,
Not gallop with the eight steeds, neighing at their head?

In these disordered times, where can such a horse be
        found?
Only in dark clouds and thick vapours does such purity
        descend.
Recently a proclamation was published in the capital,
Will this Ch'i-lin be permitted still to walk the earth?

~

[48]

ALISON BRACKENBURY

FROM

Breaking Ground
~

Facing the window, whose red iron rusts,
see horses fade; slow stirring now, they blur
the waves of light. Starred heads shift by a gate;
lifting briefly – not old power;
freedom, a rough offer. Who accepts?

In these closed spaces, tied, they live with men,
brushed and fed and schooled. They are built courses
for races, jumping. Hands which lead them through
barred doors, caress them: dark feet kick them.

Men half-made my horses.

Who made you?

~

[49]

ANONYMOUS

The Adam and Eve of the Mustangs: Texas 1540

~

The Spanish camp lies sleeping
    The horses hobbled and fed,
And by his fire the sentry droops
    With Aragon in his head.

The captain enters kingdoms,
    The soldiers finger gold,
But the Spanish horses stamp and sweat
    In the dreamed-of galleon hold.

They whinny for far-off pasturage
    And farther desert sands,
For the white-robed desert riders
    With naked heels and hands;

Their days of freer journeying
    Have never been forgot
The saddle-bags being heavy
    And the gilded trappings hot.

The gilded trappings irksome
    And the rider closed in steel,
With conquest on the bridle
    And agony at his heel.

. . . Snap! Like a bough in winter
    Abruptly from the tree,
The Arab stallion's broken
His tether to go free.

He stretches to the gallop
    And feels the prairie grasses
Crisply give to his going
    And spring up as he passes;

A wind from the western mountains
    Tangles his wayward mane;
He caracules where no other hooves
    Have touched the naked plain,

And all night flees. At morning
    He wheels around to stare
Where with light step following
    He sees the Barbary mare.

~

G. A. BRANT

A Gift to Man

~

When God created Horses
So my Father did maintain,
   He took some tireless muscle
And mingled it with brain.

   He added grace and carriage
And a sure foot, agile gait,
   With a sense of noble bearing
And courage as a trait.

   Then He used these ingredients
To meet His master plan.
   When His creation was completed
He gave this wonderous gift to man.

~

THE KORAN

~

When God had created the horse,
He spoke to the magnificent creature:
'I have made thee unlike any other.
All the treasures of this earth lie between thine eyes.
Thou shall cast mine enemies beneath thine hooves,
But thou shall carry my friends on thy back.

This shall be the seat
From whence praises rise unto Me.
Thou shall find happiness all over the earth,
And thou shall be favoured above all other creatures,
For to thee shall accrue the love of the master of the earth.
Thou shall fly without wings
And conquer without sword.'

≈

[52]

ANONYMOUS
A Horse's Prayer

≈

Going up hill whip me not.
Going down hill hurry me not.
On level road spare me not.
Loose in stable forget me not.
Of hay and corn rob me not.
Of clean water rob me not.
Of sponge and brush neglect me not.
Of soft dry bed deprive me not.
Tired or hot, wash me not.
In sick or cold, chill me not.
With bits and reins, Oh! jerk me not.
And when you're angry
Oh! strike me not!

≈

RONALD DUNCAN

The Horse

～

Where in this wide world can man find
Nobility without pride,
Friendship without envy,
Or beauty without vanity?
Here, where grace is laced with muscle
And strength by gentleness confined.

He serves without servility:
He has fought without enmity:
There is nothing so powerful,
Nothing less violent;
There is nothing so quick;
Nothing more patient.

England's past has been borne on his back,
All our history is his industry;
We are his heirs,
He is our inheritance.
Ladies and Gentlemen
THE HORSE.

～

WILLIAM SHAKESPEARE

FROM

King Richard III
Act V, Scene iv

~

King Richard. A horse! A horse! my kingdom for a horse!
Sir William Catesby. Withdraw, my lord; I'll help you to a
    horse.
King Richard. Slave, I have set my life upon a cast,
And I will stand the hazard of the die:
I think there be six Richmonds in the field;
Five have I slain today instead of him.
A horse! a horse! my kingdom for a horse!

~

THE BIBLE

FROM

The Book of Job
Chapter 39 Verses 20–25

~

The glory of his nostrils is terrible.

He paweth in the valley, and rejoiceth in his strength: he
goeth on to meet the armed men.

He mocketh at fear and is not affrighted; neither turneth
he back from the sword.

The quiver rattleth against him, the glittering spear and the shield.

He swalloweth the ground with fierceness and rage: neither believeth he that it is the sound of the trumpet.

He saieth among the trumpets, Ha, Ha; and he smelleth the battle afar off, the thunder of the captains, and the shouting.

～

[56]

JULIAN GRENFELL

FROM

Into Battle

～

In dreary, doubtful waiting hours,
    Before the brazen frenzy starts,
The horses show him nobler powers;
    O patient eyes, courageous hearts!

And when the burning moment breaks,
    And all things else are out of mind,
And only joy of battle takes
    Him by the throat, and makes him blind,

Through joy and blindness he shall know,
    Nor caring much to know, that still,
Nor lead nor steel shall reach him, so
    That it be not the Destined Will.

The thundering line of battle stands,
　　And in the air Death moans and sings;
But Day shall clasp him with strong hands,
　　And Night shall fold him in soft wings.

~

[57]
CONTEMPORARY RECORDS OF THE CONQUISTADORES *c.* 1525
Victory

~

After God, we owed the victory to the horses.

~

WILL H. OGILVIE
The Waler
(1916)
~

There goes a bucker, wherever they bred him,
　By the lift of his loin and the white in his eye;
Wide were the paddocks, I'll wager, that fed him;
　Red were the ridges that ran to the sky!
See how those sensitive ears of his quiver!
　See how, high-headed, the crowd he disdains,
Full of the pride of the Warrego River,
　Full of the scorn of the Irrara plains!

Bit of a rogue and a renegade is he?
　Bad to get on to and hang to and hold?
Bent like a bow does he buck till you're dizzy? –
　Thus they behave where his lordship was foaled.
Send for that chap in the tilted sombrero,
　Cleaning a chestnut and chewing a string;
No one, it may be, looks less of a hero,
　But once in the saddle he sits like a king.

The day will arrive when the war-front is wider,
　And swifter the squadrons will gallop and form;
Then give him his lean-visaged, light-handed rider
　And launch him away on the leagues of the storm;
Give him his head to the stars growing paler
　That mark where the Dawn is a symbol and sign,
And first of them all before night shall the Waler
　With foam on his muzzle drink deep of the Rhine.

~

ROBERT WAY

The Cavalry of Sybaris

~

In the good days of old, so I have heard it told,
Sybaris was rich both in silver and gold.
And its ladies were fair, with dark lustrous hair –
To its food and its wine there was none to compare.
And each knight kept, of course, a most wonderful horse,
So they made a respectable cavalry force,
Though they did not delight in the heat of the fight
Nor sought to do deeds of great daring and might.
And much stranger still, they delighted in drill
And every new movement they learnt with a will.
How to charge they forgot, but learnt the Spanish Trot
And Piaffes and things whether useful or not.
So one day at a feast, when a man from the East
Told them how they train there a strange dancing beast –
'That sounds jolly', said one, 'Don't let us be outdone
By any damn foreigner under the sun.'
So their steeds they prepare with the greatest of care
Until they had learnt to dance to any air.
Then arrangements were made and they held a parade
And the horses all danced while the flute players played.
Such outstanding success had a wonderful press.
The whole of Greece heard of the thing, more or less.
But before very long, well, something went wrong
(And the people of Croton were not very strong)
And the Sybarites decide that they've been defied
And off to do battle with Croton they ride.
When the foemen appear, they find something quite
        queer:
In the front rank is neither a sword nor a spear
But flutes, all in a row; and when they start to blow
The guile of the stratagem clearly they show.
For they all start to play a dance tune of the day

And the hearts of the Sybarites fill with dismay.
For their horses all prance, and all start to dance,
So that they can neither retreat nor advance.
In vain spurs are plied, but though bloody each side·
The horses' long training could not be denied.
Now the foes seize each rein and the struggle is vain
They could not use a lance, and in piles they were slain.
So the knights found their graves, and their wives became
       slaves,
And Sybaris' ruins are lapped by the waves.
And this is the moral: I hope that you will
Teach your soldiers to fight, to the devil with drill!

~

[60]

G. A. FOTHERGILL
To Polo

Coupled with the name of Walter Buckmaster, undisputed polo
prince, and one of the best and hardest men to hounds of any
period.

~

Our young men still may spur the heel,
    And sport 'cap', 'coat' and 'leathers', –
Compared with covering wrought of steel
    Almost as light as feathers:
Heads once were made to carry weight,
    And not to carry knowledge;
But all that's past and out of date –
    Heads now bring brains from College.

The lance exchanged for polo stick,
    The sword for cutting whip,

We catch glad sounds of willow click
    And sight good horsemanship.
It's still a mimic of war of course,
    With each one quick as a cony

Not mounted on an armoured horse
    But on a polo pony,
Not striking at a block of steel
    But at a ball of wood,
And twisting with it like an eel
    As brave as 'Robin Hood'.

And if there chance an accident –
    A 'charger' slip or fall –
It's ten to one no detriment
    To pony, man and all.
Long live the fighting polo game,
    Buckmaster with it too –
The old Cantab whose famous name
    Stands first in *Sports Who's Who*.

~

[61]

WILL H. OGILVIE
Polo Ponies
~

Beneath the rainbow silks they sail
    Like birds that wheel and cross
Then, all their speed of no avail,
Come round to bit and martingale
    With heads that reach and toss.

The ceaseless stick beside them swings,
　　The torn turf marks their track,
To heaving flanks the dark sweat clings
And from their fretted bridle rings
　　The foam comes feathering back.

But well they know there is no game
　　That men their masters play
Can fan like this their hearts to flame
And make them one with every aim
　　That fills the crowded day.

And if the sweat's on sobbing flanks,
　　And necks are lathered white,
Have they not won from Beauty's ranks
Caress and kiss and whispered thanks
　　For this their hard-fought fight?

LORD BYRON

FROM

Mazeppa

~

With flowing tail, and flying mane,
Wide nostrils – never stretch'd by pain,
Mouths bloodless to the bit or rein,
And feet that iron never shod,
And flanks unscarr'd by spur or rod.
A thousand horse, the wild, the free,
Like waves that follow o'er the sea,
Came quickly thundering on.

~

[63]

THE KORAN

~

By the snorting chargers!
Those that dash off sparks of fire!
And scour to the attack at morn!
Stirring therein the dust aloft
And clearing their midway through
A host.

~

[64]

ANONYMOUS

~

Look back at our struggle for freedom,
Trace our present day's strength to its source;
And you'll find that man's pathway to glory
Is strewn with the bones of a horse.

~

[65]

ANONYMOUS

Memorial at the Church of St Jude, Hampstead

~

In grateful and reverent memory of the Empire's horses
(some 375,000) who fell in the Great War (1914–1918).
Most obediently, and often most painfully, they died.

'Faithful unto death not one of them is forgotten
before God.'

~

MATTHEW ARNOLD

FROM

Balder Dead

The Valkyries were beautiful maidens whose job it was to rescue
dying Vikings and take them to Valhalla. The horses are supposed
to be impersonations of the clouds with dew and frost dropping
from their manes.

~

There through some battle-field, where men fall fast,
Their horses fetlock-deep in blood, they ride,
And pick the bravest warriors out for death,
Whom they bring back with them at night to Heaven
To glad the Gods, and feast in Odin's hall.

~

[67]

HOMER

FROM

The Iliad
Book X lines 638–69

~

With words of friendship and extended hands
They greet the kings; and Nestor first demands:
'Say thou, whose praises all our host proclaim,
Thou living glory of the Grecian name!
Say whence these coursers? by what chance bestow'd,
The spoil of foes, or present of a god?
Not those fair steeds, so radiant and so gay,

That draw the burning chariot of the day.
Old as I am, to age I scorn to yield,
And daily mingle in the martial field;
But sure till now no coursers struck my sight
Like these, conspicuous through the ranks of fight.
Some god, I deem, conferr'd the glorious prize,
Bless'd as ye are, and favourites of the skies;
The care of him who bids the thunder roar,
And her, whose fury bathes the world with gore.'
'Father! not so, (sage Ithacus rejoin'd,)
The gifts of heaven are of a nobler kind.
Of Thracian lineage are the steeds ye view
Whose hostile king the brave Tydides slew.'
. . .
Then o'er the trench the bounding coursers flew;
The joyful Greeks with loud acclaim pursue.
Straight to Tydides' high pavilion borne,
The matchless steeds his ample stalls adorn:
The neighing coursers their new fellows greet,
And the full racks are heap'd with generous wheat.

~

[68]

ANONYMOUS

FROM

Gereint Son of Erbin

TRANSLATED BY
Gwyn Williams

~

Before Gereint, the enemy's punisher,
I saw white stallions with red shins
and after the war-cry a bitter grave.

Before Gereint, the enemy's depriver,
I saw stallions red-shinned from battle
and after the war-cry a bitter pensiveness.

Before Gereint, scourge of the enemy,
I saw stallions girdled in white
and after the war-cry a bitter covering.

. . .

There were fast horses under Gereint's thigh,
long-shanked, wheat-fed;
they were red, in their rush like milky eagles.

There were fast horses under Gereint's thigh,
long-shanked, grain nourished them;
they were red, their rush like black eagles.

There were fast horses under Gereint's thigh,
long-shanked, devourers of grain;
They were red, their rush like red eagles.

There were fast horses under Gereint's thigh,
long-shanked, emptiers of grain;
they were red, their rush like white eagles.

There were fast horses under Gereint's thigh,
long-shanked, with the stride of a stag,
like the roar of burning on a waste mountain.

There were fast horses under Gereint's thigh,
long-shanked, greedy for grain,
blue-gray, their hair tipped with silver.

There were fast horses under Gereint's thigh,
long-shanked, seizing on grain;
they were red, their rush like grey eagles.

≈

THE BIBLE

TWO VERSES FROM

The Book of Revelation
Chapter 6 verse 8

~

And I looked, and behold a pale horse:
and his name that sat on him was Death.

Chapter 19 verse 11

~

And I saw Heaven opened, and behold a white horse;
and he that sat upon him was called Faithful and True.

~

TU FU

A White Horse

TRANSLATED BY
Richard King

~

The white horse has come from the North-East
His empty saddle pierced by two arrows.

Let us pity the officer who rode him,
We shall not see his gallantry again!

The Chief Commander was recently killed,
Attacked at Shang-chou at dead of night;
There are so many ways to die in rebellions,
Alas, I sigh, my tears pour down.

~

[71]

JOHN COVERNTON
White Horses
~

I saw white horses
And horsemen gathering
Out at sea.
Line upon line,
A thousand pennants streaming,
They showed their strength.
Galloping fast
Knee to knee,
Their horses tightly curbed,
Their armour gleaming
And foam flecked white.
I heard the sound
Of a distant rumbling;
And then hooves as
Horse after horse,
As far as the sky beyond,
Approaching ever nearer
In cloud patched sunlight,
Nearer and nearer,

They rode into shallow water.
I held my breath as
One by one
Each horse touched sand,
And stumbling
Fell forward on the shore.
I looked again,
The leading horse
And horseman both had gone,
And trailing at my feet
Lay the ermine border of
The cloak that he had worn.

~

[72]

ROY CAMPBELL

Horses on the Camargue

~

In the grey wastes of dread,
The haunt of shattered gulls where nothing moves
But in a shroud of silence like the dead,
I heard a sudden harmony of hooves,
And, turning, saw afar
A hundred snowy horses unconfined,
The silver runaways of Neptune's car
Racing, spray-curled, like waves before the wind.
Sons of the Mistral, fleet
As him with whose strong gusts they love to flee,
Who shod the flying thunders of their feet
And plumed them with the snortings of the sea;
Theirs is no earthly breed
Who only haunt the verges of the earth

And only on the sea's salt herbage feed –
Surely the great white breakers gave them birth.
For when for years a slave,
A horse of the Camargue, in alien lands,
Should catch some far-off fragrance of the wave
Carried far inland from his native sands,
Many have told the tale
Of how in fury, foaming at the rein,
He hurls his rider; and with lifted tail,
With coal-red eyes and cataracting mane,
Heading his course for home,
Though sixty foreign leagues before him sweep,
Will never rest until he breathes the foam
And hears the native thunder of the deep.
But when the great gusts rise
And lash their anger on these arid coasts,
When the scared gulls career with mournful cries
And whirl across the waste like driven ghosts:
When hail and fire converge,
The only souls to which they strike no pain
Are the white-crested fillies of the surge
And the white horses of the windy plain.
Then in their strength and pride
The stallions of the wildnerness rejoice;
They feel their Master's trident in their side,
And high and shrill they answer to his voice.
With white tails smoking free,
Long streaming manes, and arching necks, they show
Their kinship to their sisters of the sea –
And forward hurl their thunderbolts of snow.
Still out of hardship bred,
Spirits of power and beauty and delight
Have ever on such frugal pastures fed
And loved to course with tempests through the night.

~

[73]

GEORGE MEREDITH

FROM

The Mares of the Camargue

~

A hundred mares, all white! their manes
Like mace-reed of the marshy plains
Thick-tufted, wavy, free o' the shears:
And when the fiery squadron rears
Bursting at speed, each mane appears
Even as the white scarf of a fay
Floating upon their necks along the heavens away.

~

[74]

THOMAS MOORE

O'Donohue's Mistress

The ghost of the Chieftain O'Donohue and his white horse are
supposed to glide over Lake Killarney on May Day.

~

Of all the bright haunts, where daylight leaves
Its lingering smile on golden eves,
Fair Lake, thou'rt dearest to me;
For when the last April sun grows dim,
Thy Naiads prepare his steed for him
Who dwells, bright Lake, in thee.

Of all the proud steeds, that ever bore
Young plumed Chiefs on sea or shore,

White Steed, most joy to thee;
Who still, with the first young glance of spring,
From under that glorious lake dost bring
My love, my chief, to me.

While, white as the sail some bark unfurls,
When newly launch'd, thy long mane curls,
Fair Steed, as white and free;
And spirits, from all the lake's deep bowers,
Glide o'er the blue wave scattering flowers,
Around my love and thee.

Of all the sweet deaths that maidens die,
Whose lovers beneath the cold waves lie,
Most sweet that death will be,
Which, under the next May evening's light,
When thou and thy steed are lost to sight,
Dear love, I'll die for thee.

～

[75]

LAURENCE HOUSMAN
To a Rider Drowned at Sea
～

Leader, and lover of speed and the level courses
Of crowded miles, on the plain where the goal-posts stand,
Rider of horses, lord of the swift dark steed
Life, for a moment held in your sole command –
Here, in dusk is your goal: here dimly appears,
Bearing no garland aloft, your lintel of home;
Your day is done, and the rein
Of the rider has dropped from your hand.

Over your head unheeded (but loud in my ears)
Go the running feet of the foam,
And the sound of the wild sea-horses –
Riderless – galloping home!

~

[76]

HOMER

On Neptune

The Ancient Greeks regarded Neptune as an equestrian deity as
well as God of the Sea.

~

Neptune, the mighty marine god, I sing;
. . .
O thou earth shaker; thy command, twofold
The gods have sorted; making thee of horses
The awful tamer, and of naval forces
The sure preserver.

~

[77]

ANONYMOUS

St Michael

TRANSLATED BY
Alexander Carmichael

In Scotland St Michael of the White Steeds was the patron saint of
the sea and of horses and horsemen – the Gaelic Neptune. This is
from a collection of Scottish customs, *Carmina Gadelica.*

~

Thou wert the warrior of courage
Going on the journey of prophecy,
Thou wouldst not travel on a cripple,
Though didst take the steed of the god Michael,
He was without bit in his mouth,
Thou didst ride him on the wing,
Thou didst leap over the knowledge of Nature.

~

[78]

ANONYMOUS

~

There are steeds on the Border and steeds in the West,
And Ireland's green isle layeth claim to the best,
And I've seen in their princely and elegant garb
The fast-going Arab and high-mettled Barb.

~

ROBERT SOUTHEY

FROM

The Curse of Kehama
The Sacrifice

This is a description of a sacrificial horse in the ancient Brahmin tradition. Much reverence was given to the victim before the sacrifice.

∼

Along the mead the hallow'd Steed
Still wanders whereso'er he will,
  O'er hill, or dale, or plain;
No human hand hath trick'd that mane
From which he shakes the morning dew;
  His mouth has never felt the rein,
His lips have never froth'd the chain;
  For pure of blemish and of stain,
His neck unbroke to mortal yoke,
Like Nature free the Steed must be,
  Fit offering to the Immortals he.
A year and a day the Steed must stray
Wherever chance may guide his way,
  Before he fall at Seeva's shrine.

∼

LI PO

The Heavenly Horse

TRANSLATED BY
Richard King

～

The Heavenly Horse has come from the caves of the
      Yueh-shih
Tiger-markings on his back, bones to support a dragon's
      wings.
Neighs at the black clouds
And shakes his dark mane.
With fine muscles and great stamina, he runs so fast he
      makes no sound.

Springing up K'un-lun,
Crossing the Western borders,
His four feet never stumble.
Groomed in Yen at cock-crow, he can be fed in Yueh by
      afternoon,
A fabulous stride, swift as lightning, his legs a blur of speed.

The Heavenly Horse neighs,
The Fei-huang hastens.
His eye bright as Venus, his spirit soaring like a pair of ducks,
His tail a comet, his head erect and proud,
Red saliva glistening, streams of red sweat flowing.
He has gone with the dragon-horses, galloping the Heavenly
      Highway.

A golden moon on his halter reflects the starry city,
Eagerly he gallops on, soaring over the nine states.
Who would dare to sell him for a pile of white jade badges?
He looks back and laughs at you purple swallows
He alone knows how stupid you all are.

The Heavenly Horse gallops,
Longing for his master's carriage.
A flick of the reins to urge him forward, and the floating clouds
        disperse.
After ten thousand li his feet drag,
He gazes up at the distant Ch'ang-ho gate.
If he does not meet master Han Feng
Who will pick him out as a descendant of the hurrying shadow

There are white clouds in the blue sky
The hills tower up in the distance.
The salt cart goes up a steep slope
He staggers but is forced on. I fear it may be too late.

Po Lo looked after him, after he was left by the road,
He wore out his strength in youth, and is rejected in old age.
If only he could meet T'ien Tzu-fang
He would take pity on him for me.
Even the crops that grow on the Jade Mountain
Could not satisfy his desperate hunger.

The fierce frosts of the fifth month shrivelled the cassia twigs.
Broken-in and long-suffering, his eyebrows knit together.
I beg you to redeem him and give him to Emperor Hu
So that he also can dance in the shadows at Yao-chih.

DOROTHY WELLESLEY

FROM

Horses

❦

Who, in the garden-pony carrying skeps
Of grass or fallen leaves, his knees gone slack,
Round belly, hollow back,
Sees the Mongolian Tarpan of the Steppes?
Or, in the Shire with plaits and feathered feet,
The war-horse like the wind the Tartar knew?
Or, in the Suffolk Punch, spells out anew
The wild grey asses fleet
With stripe from head to tail and moderate ears?
In cross sea-donkeys, sheltering as storm gathers,
The mountain zebras maned upon the withers,
With round enormous ears?

And who in thoroughbreds in stable garb
Of blazoned rug, ranged orderly, will mark
The wistful eyelashes so long and dark,
And call to mind the old blood of the Barb?
And that slim island on whose bare campaigns
Galloped with flying manes
For a King's pleasure, churning surf and scud,
A white Arabian stud?

That stallion, teazer to Hobgoblin, free
And foaled upon a plain of Barbary:
Godolphin Barb, who dragged a cart for hire
In Paris, but became a famous sire,
Covering all lovely mares, and she who threw
Rataplan to the Baron, loveliest shrew;
King Charles's royal mares; The Dodsworth Dam;
And the descendants: Yellow Turk, King Tom;
And Lath out of Roxana, famous foal;

Careless; Eclipse, unbeaten in the race,
With white blaze on his face;
Prunella who was dam to Parasol.

Blood Arab, pony, pedigree, no name,
All horses are the same:
The Shetland stallion stunted by the damp,
Yet filled with self-importance, stout and small;
The Cleveland slow and tall;
New Forests that may ramp
Their lives out, being branded, breeding free
When bluebells turn the Forest to a sea,
When mares with foal at foot flee down the glades,
Sheltering in bramble coverts
From mobs of corn-fed lovers;
Or, at the acorn harvest, in stockades
A round-up being afoot, will stand at bay,
Or, making for the heather clearings, splay
Wide-spread towards the bogs by gorse and whin,
Roped as they flounder in
By foresters.

. . .

Patient, adventurous still,
A horse's ears bob on the distant hill;
He starts to hear
A pheasant chuck or whirr, having the fear
In him of ages filled with war and raid,
Night gallop, ambuscade;
Remembering adventures of his kin
With giant winged worms that coiled round mountain
            bases,
And Nordic tales of young gods riding races
Up courses of the rainbow . . .

~

G. G. SILL

FROM

Hawking
A Lay Dedicated to St Hubert

~

Thro' the castle gates first ride they forth,
    A glittering gallant band,
Renowned knights, whose falchions bright
Have earned them laurels in many a fight,
    In a strange and distant land.

And maidens, too, on palfreys gay,
    From Araby, so rare
Snorting and prancing on they bound –
So light, they scarcely touch the ground –
    A beauteous sight they were!

Swift as the wind, fast on they go,
    O'er hill and valley wide;
With falcons fierce and gos-hawks fair,
Their bewits tinkling shrill and clear,
    How bonnily they ride!

~

W. S. MERWIN

Two Horses

~

Oh in whose grove have we wakened, the bees
Still droning under the carved wall, the fountain playing
Softly to itself, and the gold light, muted,
Moving long over the olives; and whose,
Stamping the shadowy grass at the end of the garden,
Are these two wild horses tethered improbably
To the withes of a young quince? No rider
Is to be seen; they bear neither saddle nor bridle;
Their brute hooves splash the knee-high green
Without sound, and their flexed tails like flags float,
Whipping, their brows down like bulls. Yet the small tree
Is not shaken; and the broken arches
Of their necks in the dim air are silent
As the doorways of ruins. Birds flit in the garden:
Jay and oriole, blades in the hanging shadows,
Small cries confused. And dawn would be eastward
Over the dark neck a red mane tossed high
Like flame, and the dust brightening along the wall.
These have come up from Egypt, from the dawn countries,
Syria, and the land between the rivers,
Have ridden at the beaks of vessels, by Troy neighed,
And along the valley of the Danube, and to Etruria;
And all dust was of their making; and passion
Under their hooves puffed into flight like a sparrow
And died down when they departed. The haze of summer
Blows south over the garden terraces,
Vague through the afternoon, remembering rain;
But in the night green with beasts as April with grass
Orion would hunt high from southward, over the hill,
And the blood of beasts herald morning. Where these
                    have passed,
Tramping white roads, their ears drinking the sword-crash,

The chariots are broken, bright battle-cars
Shambles under earth; whether by sharp bronze
Or the years' ebbing, all blood has flowed into the ground;
There was wailing at sundown, mourning for kings,
Weeping of widows, but these went faint, were forgotten,
And the columns have fallen like shadows. Crickets
Sing under the stones; and beyond the carved wall
Westward, fires drifting in darkness like the tails
Of jackals flaring, no hounds heard at their hunting,
Float outward into the dark. And these horses stamp
Before us now in this garden; and northward
Beyond the terraces the misted sea
Swirls endless, hooves of the gray wind forever
Thundering, churning the ragged spume-dusk
High that there be no horizons nor stars, and there
Are white islands riding, ghost-guarded, twisted waves
        flashing,
Porpoises plunging like the necks of horses.

~

[84]

EDEN PHILLPOTTS

The Cart-Horses
~

'Twixt two and three upon a silent night,
As earth rolled dreaming in the full morn tide,
Slow hooves came thud and thud: there hove in sight
Black horses twain, that wandered side by side,
Two great cart-horses, looming giant large,
Enjoyed their rest. Each to the other spoke,
Then stood and drank beside a streamlet's marge,
While moonlight found their lustrous eyes and woke
A glint of consciousness, a hint of mind.

Now they rubbed noses, shook their heavy manes,
Lifted their necks and neighed upon the wind,
Then fell to whispering, their little brains
Busy about shared interests, unshared
By those for whom their strenuous time was spent.
On something said, whereat the other stared,
Then started galloping, and off they went,
To vanish on the far night-hidden heath;
And well I knew they were exchanging thought,
Uttering strange, dim things with their sweet breath
Of which we busy, daylight folk know nought –
Views touching fate, under the still moonshine,
As near to truth, perchance, as yours, or mine.

~

[85]

ROBIN IVY

~

Horses under
An oak
Exchange secrets.

~

[86]

NIKOLAI ALEKSEEVICH ZABOLOTSKY
The Face of the Horse

TRANSLATED BY
Daniel Weissbort

~

Animals do not sleep. At night
They stand over the world like a stone wall.

The cow's retreating head
Rustles the straw with its smooth horns,
The rocky brow a wedge
Between the age-old cheek bones,
And the mute eyes
Turning sluggishly.

There's more intelligence and beauty in the horse's face.
He hears the talk of leaves and stones.
Intent, he knows the animal's cry
And the nightingale's murmur in the copse.

And knowing all, to whom may he recount
His wonderful visions?
The night is hushed. In the dark sky
Constellations rise.
The horse stands like a knight keeping watch,
The wind plays in his light hair,
His eyes burn like two huge worlds,
And his mane lifts like the imperial purple.

And if a man should see
The horse's magical face,
He would tear out his own impotent tongue
And give it to the horse. For
This magical creature is surely worthy of it.
Then we should hear words.
Words large as apples. Thick
As honey or buttermilk.
Words which penetrate like flame
And, once within the soul, like fire in some hut,
Illuminate its wretched trappings.
Words which do not die
And which we celebrate in song.

But now the stable is empty,
The trees have dispersed,
Pinch-faced morning has swaddled the hills,
Unlocked the fields for work.
And the horse, caged within its shafts,
Dragging a covered wagon,
Gazes out of its meek eyes
Upon the enigmatic, stationary world.

≈

TED HUGHES

A Dream of Horses

~

We were born grooms, in stable-straw we sleep still,
All our wealth horse-dung and the combings of horses,
And all we can talk about is what horses ail.

Out of the night that gulfed beyond the palace-gate
There shook hooves and hooves and hooves of horses:
Our horses battered their stalls; their eyes jerked white.

And we ran out, mice in our pockets and straw in our hair,
Into darkness that was avalanching to horses
And a quake of hooves. Our lantern's little orange flare

Made a round mask of our each sleep-dazed face,
Bodiless, or else bodies by horses
That whinnied and bit and cannoned the world from its
        place.

The tall palace was so white, the moon was so round,
Everything else this plunging of horses
To the rim of our eyes that strove for the shapes of the sound.

We crouched at our lantern, our bodies drank the din,
And we longed for a death trampled by such horses
As every grain of the earth had hooves and mane.

We must have fallen like drunkards into a dream
Of listening, lulled by the thunder of the horses.
We awoke stiff; broad day had come.

Out through the gate the unprinted desert stretched
To stone and scorpion; our stable-horses
Lay in their straw, in a hag-sweat, listless and wretched.

Now let us, tied, be quartered by these poor horses,
If but doomsday's flames be great horses,
The forever itself a circling of the hooves of horses.

~

[88]

CHRISTOPHER FRY

FROM
Venus Observed

~

Horses, it always seems
To me, are half a dream, even when
You have them under your hand, and when I *dream* them
They tremble and sweat, the caves of their nostrils blowing
Bright clouds of breath, a foaming sea
Breaks against their mouths, their flanks are smoking
Like Abel's fire to heaven, as though
A dreadful necessity had ridden them hard
Through the miles of my sleep, all the benighted way
From legend into life. And then in the morning
There they are in the stables, waiting to be blessed.

~

WALTER DE LA MARE

FROM

Dreams

~

Ask not the Dreamer! See him run,
Listening a shrill and gentle neigh,
Foot into stirrup, he is up, he has won
Enchanted foothills far away.
Somewhere? Nowhere? Who need say?
So be it in secrecy of his mind
He some rare delectation find.

~

[90]

RUDYARD KIPLING

FROM

The Way Through the Woods

~

You will hear the beat of a horse's feet,
    And the swish of a skirt in the dew,
    Steadily cantering through
The misty solitudes,
    As though they perfectly knew
The old lost road through the woods –
But there is no road through the woods!

~

ANONYMOUS

The Midnight Steeplechase

~

The steam of their steeds,
Like a mist of the meads,
Veiled the moon in a curtain of cloud.
And the stars so bright
Shuddered in light
As the unhallowed troop in their shadowy shroud,
Galloping, whooping, and yelling aloud,
Fast and unfailing, furious in flight,
Rattled on like a hailstorm, and vanished in night.

~

[92]

THOMAS BABINGTON MACAULAY

FROM

Lays of Ancient Rome
The Battle of Lake Regillus

Castor and Pollux, the twin equestrian gods, were said to have
helped the Romans at the Battle of Lake Regillus, mounted on two
white horses. They then took the news of the victory to the City
and vanished.

~

Then burst from that great concourse
    A shout that shook the towers,
And some ran north, and some ran south,
    Crying, 'The day is ours!'
But on rode these strange horsemen,

With slow and lordly pace;
And none who saw their bearing
    Durst ask their name or race.
On rode they to the Forum,
    While laurel boughs and flowers,
From house tops and from windows,
    Fell on their crests in showers.
When they drew nigh to Vesta,
    They vaulted down amain,
And washed their horses in the well
    That springs by Vesta's fane.
And straight again they mounted,
    And rode to Vesta's door;
Then, like a blast, away they passed,
    And no man saw them more.

~

[93]

DAVID CAMPBELL

The Stockman

~

The sun was in the summer grass,
The coolibahs were twisted steel;
The stockman paused beneath their shade
And sat upon his heel,
And with the reins looped through his arm
He rolled tobacco in his palm.

His horse stood still. His cattle-dog
Tongued in the shadow of the tree,
And for a moment on the plain
Time waited for the three.
And then the stockman licked his fag
And Time took up his solar swag.

I saw the stockman mount and ride
Across the mirage on the plain;
And still that timeless moment brought
Fresh ripples to my brain:
It seemed in that distorting air
I saw his grandson sitting there.

~

[94]

G. A. FOTHERGILL

FROM

The Recollection of a Westmorland Coach-Horn

~

Honour to the coats of red
Donned by drivers long since dead!
Honour to the teams they drove!
Each with each for glory strove.
Gone, the leaders' duplex will –
Gone, the springing at the hill;
Gone, the tugging at the pole
By the wheelers as they stole
Bravely downwards to the dale,
Bringing safe the welcome mail;
Gone the handly stableman;
Gone complete, the coaching clan:
All have hurried past the post, –
Honour to the phantom host!

~

[95]

LES MURRAY

FROM

The Tube

~

. . . It would have worked
and brought the Melbourne Cup alive
To Ballarat, which was his object –
but no one had yet sent an aerial wave
and wire had this defect;

signals couldn't race so fast
along it that they'd sustain a picture.
Only when the horse-drawn age was past
could horses surge into the air
with music and gunfire, galloping broadcast.

~

[96]

SID DELANY

A Horse in the City

~

'You can keep your buses and cars,
I'll take a horse.'
            'A horse?'
              'Yes.'
                'Don't be mad;
What would you do with a horse?'
            'Ride it, of course.

You know where I'd ride? I'd ride to the park
And beyond, by the beach, to the hills
And along through the scrub to a place I know
Where a thin little rivulet spills;
And I'd sit in the saddle and dream some dreams,
And after a while I'd take
To a winding trail that I rode as a boy
To the edge of the moonlit lake . . .
I'd ride to the end of the world of trees
And the horse could set the pace
As long as I had the sky and the stars
And the night wind in my face.'
'If you had a horse. Why, you can't ride.'
'I can.'
        But the fellow laughed,
'And where in the city would you keep a horse
If you had a horse? You're daft.'

~

[97]

WILL H. OGILVIE

FROM

The Horseman

~

Let oil, nor steam, nor wings of dream deprive us of our
        own –
The wide world for a kingdom and the saddle for a
        throne!

~

LES MURRAY

FROM

Barrenjoey

~

Where the poet Brennan wandered
the soaked steeps of his mind
now men and women warily
strike deals that can't be signed.
Where once in salt sheet-iron days
a girl might halt her filly
under posies atop cornstalks three yards high,
groves of the Gymea lily,
the northward sandstone finger, knobbed
with storms and strange injections
has beckoned Style, and Porsche windscreens
glimmer with cool deflections –

~

EDWIN MUIR

FROM

The Horses

~

And then, that evening
Late in the summer the strange horses came.
We heard a distant tapping on the road,
A deepening drumming; it stopped, went on again
And at the corner changed to hollow thunder.

We saw the heads
Like a wild wave charging and were afraid.
We had sold our horses in our fathers' time
To buy new tractors. Now they were strange to us
As fabulous steeds set on an ancient shield
Or illustrations in a book of knights.
We did not dare go near them. Yet they waited,
Stubborn and shy, as if they had been sent
By an old command to find our whereabouts
And that long-lost archaic companionship.
In the first moment we had never a thought
That they were creatures to be owned and used.
Among them were some half-a-dozen colts
Dropped in some wilderness of the broken world,
Yet new as if they had come from their own Eden.
Since then they have pulled our ploughs and borne our
        loads,
But that free servitude still can pierce our hearts.
Our life is changed; their coming our beginning.

~

[100]

V. SACKVILLE WEST

FROM

The Land
The Yeoman

~

He tills the soil today,
Surly and grave, his difficult wage to earn.
Cities of discontent, the sickened nerve,
Are still a fashion that he will not learn.
His will is still the obstinate old way,

Even though his horses stare above the hedge,
And whinny, while the tractor drives its wedge
Where they were wont to serve,
And iron robs them of their privilege.
Still in his heart not given
To such encroachments on a natural creed;
Not wholly given, though he bows to need
By urgency and competition driven,
And vanity, to follow with the tide.
Still with secret triumph he will say,
'Tractor for sand, maybe, but horse for clay.'

~

[101]

FRANCES CORNFORD
Cambridgeshire
~

The stacks, like blunt impassive temples, rise
Across flat fields against the autumnal skies.
The hairy-hoovèd horses plough the land,
Or as in prayer and meditation stand
Upholding square, primeval, dung-stained carts,
With an unending patience in their hearts.

Nothing is changed. The farmer's gig goes by
Against the horizon. Surely, the same sky,
So vast and yet familiar, grey and mild,
And streaked with light like music, I, a child
Lifted my face from leaf-edged lanes to see,
Late-coming home, to bread-and-butter tea.

~

EDWIN MUIR

Horses

~

Those lumbering horses in the steady plough,
On the brown field – I wonder why, just now,
They seemed so terrible, so wild and strange,
Like magic power on the stony grange.

Perhaps some childish hour has come again,
When I watched fearful through the blackening rain
Their hooves like pistons in an ancient mill
Move up and down, yet seem as standing still.

Their conquering hooves which trod the stubble down
Were ritual which turned the field to brown,
And their great hulks were seraphim of gold,
Or mute ecstatic monsters on the mould.

And oh, the rapture when, one furrow done,
They marched broad-breasted to the sinking sun!
The light flowed off their bossy sides in flakes,
The furrows rolled behind like struggling snakes.

But when at dusk with steaming nostrils home
They came, they seemed gigantic in the gloam,
And warm and glowing with mysterious fire
Which lit their smouldering bodies on the mire.

Their eyes as brilliant and as wide as night
Gleamed with a cruel apocalyptic sight,
Their manes the leaping ire of the wind
Lifted with rage invisible and blind.

Ah! now it fades! and I must pine
Again for that dread country crystalline,

Where the blank field and the still-standing tree
Were bright and fearful presences to me.

~

[103]

THOMAS HARDY

In Time of 'The Breaking of Nations'

~

I

Only a man harrowing clods
   In a slow silent walk
With an old horse that stumbles and nods
   Half asleep as they stalk.

II

Only thin smoke without flame
   From the heaps of couch-grass;
Yet this will go onward the same
   Though Dynasties pass.

III

Yonder a maid and her wight
   Come whispering by:
War's annals will cloud into night
   Ere their story die.

~

DAVID B. NIXON

FROM

Tribute Due

~

How can you know?
Stomping long furrows
in the wake
of mighty horses,
to break the spine
of stubborn plough
with diamond dog-tooth drags.
Breasting the hill
with blaze of burnished brass
and proud plumes nodding.
Pivoting on headlands
their feet like iron
dinner plates,
as delicate as dancers.
How can you know
whose way has ever been
beyond the hedge?

~

LILIAN BOWES LYON
Ploughing
~

Early and pregnant hour;
   Hazily sunbeams lacquer
The flanks of horses ploughing the Fourteen Acre.
   They move in a cocoon of golden steam,
The logical furrow following furled and spare.
I saw the countryman tough behind his team,
   And paused to stare
At his long shadow in time, his tangent power.

~

WILFRED HOWE-NURSE
The Ploughman
~

Give me shire-bred team to follow,
   Ploughing tackle taut and strong.
Up the rise and down the hollow,
   Framm'ard, toward, all day long.

Give me sound of brasses ringing,
   Creaking whipples, jingling chains.
Give me sound of skylark singing,
   Lost to sight her song remains.

Give me scent of squitch fires burning,
    Clover flowers by land's end grown.
Give me scent of new earth turning,
    Scent of wild mint trampled down.

Give me sight of brown earth heeling
    Back from share and coulter's thrust.
Give me sight of plovers wheeling,
    Sight of kestrel's hov'ring lust.

Give me shire-bred team to follow,
    Ploughing tackle taut and strong.
Up the rise and down the hollow,
    Framm'ard, toward, all day long.

≈

[107]

WILL H. OGILVIE

FROM

Clydesdales
≈

To each the favourite of his heart,
    To each his chosen breed,
In gig and saddle, plough and cart
    To serve his separate need!
Blue blood for him who races,
    Clean limbs for him who rides,
But for me the giant graces,
And the white and honest faces,
      The power upon the traces,
        Of the Clydes!

≈

CLAUDE COLEER ABBOTT
Stallion

~

Round by the black barn and the shrunken pond
Now treading slow, now sideling proudly on,
Through warm air startled by his eager neigh
The Suffolk stallion cleaves his stately way.

His body gleaming firm as moulded bronze,
His feathered fetlocks plumed with silken gold,
His belted tail, thick mane, with ribands blent,
He strides to mate his mares, magnificent.

The deep expectant eyes shine mildly bright,
The rich flanks quiver, stiff the great neck curves,
Faster the mighty head throws toss and fling
When stabled mares whinny their welcoming.

With dull and sullen face, thin buskined legs,
Leading his charge in apathy and ease,
A dusty groom plods wearily beside
This majesty of limb, this fruitful pride.

~

WILL H. OGILVIE
The Stallion

~

Beside the dusty road he steps at ease;
His great head bending to the stallion-bar,
Now lifted, now flung downward to his knees,
Tossing the forelock from his forehead star;
Champing the while his heavy bit in pride
And flecking foam upon his flank and side.

Save for his roller striped in white and blue
He bears no harness on his mighty back;
For all the splendour of his bone and thew
He travels burdenless along the track,
Yet shall he give a hundred hefty sons
The strength to carry what his kingship shuns.

The pheasants rustling on the roadside bank,
The pigeons swinging out in sudden chase,
Break not his broad shoe's rhythmic clank
Nor set him swerving from his measured pace.
He knows the road and all its hidden fears,
His the staid calm that comes with conquering years.

He snatches at the clover as he goes,
Clinking the bit-chain as he gathers toll;
He sniffs the speedwell, through wide nostrils blows,
And but for chain and bar would kneel and roll.
His eyes alone reveal in smouldering fire
Pride held in leash, reined Lust and curbed Desire.

~

LES MURRAY

FROM

The Assimilation of Background

~

. . . Only the dog's very patient
Claws ticked with us out of the gloom
to the ground's muffling dust, to the machine shed
black with oil and bolts, with the welder
mantis-like on its cylinder of clocks
and then to the stallion's enclosure.
The great bay horse came up to the wire,
gold flares shifting on his muscles, and stood
as one ungelded in a thousand
of his race, but imprisoned for his sex,
a gene-transmitting engine, looking at us
gravely as a spirit, out between
his brain's potent programmes . . .

~

WILL H. OGILVIE

Banshee

~

He stood there, chained to wall and rack
  With trebled steel. 'For God's own sake,'
The scared groom croaked to me, 'Stand back!
  You never know – *the chains might break!*'

Within the dim light of the stall
　　I saw the wild eyes red with hate,
And marked the deep-set halter-gall
　　That told the ceaseless strife with fate.

He heard a strange foot on the floor,
　　A strange voice in the shadows sound,
And strained his fetters with a roar
　　That shook the shed from roof to ground.

The foam upon his lips was white,
　　His bitten breast was flecked with cream.
He screamed – a soul in piteous plight –
　　Hate, fear, and anguish in the scream.

'Why keep him tortured, chained and mad,
　　And dungeoned from the daylight's gold?'
'His blood's the best we ever had,
　　And all his stock are sound and bold.'

Maybe. – I crossed the sunlit lanes,
　　And only saw, with eyes a-brim,
The torn brown breast, the trebled chains,
　　The broken heart; and wept for him.

ALISON BRACKENBURY
After the X-Ray

~

If he had stayed
in the four white walls
or alone in his patch, the untidy hedge
strewing its roses through empty hours
he would never have met the dark mare
whose neck he licked by the elderflower
whose kick snapped his straight cannonbone.

For sixteen weeks he must stand in the straw
watching the light wash and ebb.
All warmth will have flowed past when he stumbles out
November's wind raw on his leg.
Was it worth it? He shuffles, he cranes to the lane,
calls her, and calls her again.

~

PETER CORNISH
Darkling

~

Chucks up his head at the barn's end
Pulls back
Black at the ring
Waits for me
To shoot bolts

Dulcet irony
To teach manners

Royal displeasure
To raise each foot a steely second early
Showing the yahoo late
A princely trick
Played with finesse
To cut converse

I am to dress but not address
Bend
To curry favour

Strange labour
That hand-dandy I attend such whimsy
Childish
But he's not a child
He's not a king
Damn it: he's a horse

Last week he bit the Irish lad
At the heath's edge dropped a girl
Cantered wild
Returned alone
Sent Yorky with a wicked hind
Visiting the muck hill

Yet when I see, after uncounted strokes
Arabian lashes fall
Or note the catlike arch of that Corinthian
          neck
Or hear at last the ransomed sigh drawn softly
          upward
From a deep imperial chest
When perfumed breath commends me
Or his head dubs my shoulder

I know only –
Beyond pride's last parados –
Joy
Not to be dismissed
That I may do

~

[114]

G. A. FOTHERGILL

Home from Hunting – Hints to Young Stablemen
~

Lead him in carefully on to his bed,
Slacken his girths and unbridle his head;
Bring him some water but not too much,
Give him a handful of hay to touch.
Get him to stale by shaking some straw
Under his belly from hind to fore,
And whistle and wait, whistle and wait –
Tired though you be and it's ever so late.
Slap both hands with your weight on his back
Where the saddle was seated – smack, smack, smack!
Rub him quite dry with a little loose straw, –
And while you are doing it shut the door;
And if he breaks out again rub, rub him more, –
Horses badly conditioned or suffering pain
Will sometimes dry off and break out again.
Rub him against the hair of his coat,
Drying to tune of a hissing note;
See that your will and your weight's in the friction,
And never you smile at an old hand's diction.

Look to his ears and belly and flanks,
Pass your hand up and down all his four shanks;
Put on his blankets and bandage his legs,
Leaving him warm as a sitting of eggs.
Mix him a mash and give it him cool,
Follow it up with a manger full:
Crushed oats with hay-chaff in stable must tell,
Horses will eat their corn slowly and well.

~

[115]

EDRIC ROBERTS
Stable Memories

~

In all the strange uncertainties of War,
    And sudden unexpected happenings,
How much, how very much, the greater store
    We set upon the dear, familiar things:
A long, lean head above a stable-door;
    The stable-yard and whirr of pigeons' wings;
A shaft of sunlight slanting through a stall;
    The smell of straw and stable odours blend
To conjure huntings days beyond recall;
    The stamp of hoofs and other sounds which send
Our hearts into our throats, but most of all,
    The whickering in greeting of a friend.

~

DYLAN THOMAS

Fern Hill

~

And then to awake, and the farm, like a wanderer white
With the dew, come back, the cock on his shoulder: it was all
   Shining, it was Adam and maiden,
    The sky gathered again
   And the sun grew round that very day.
So it must have been after the birth of the simple light
In the first, spinning place, the spellbound horses walking warm
Out of the whinnying green stable
On to the fields of praise.

~

EDRIC ROBERTS

Out at Grass

~

Like figures cut in a silhouette,
   A group of hunters, beneath the trees,
Stands idle, save for the constant fret
   Of manes and tails in the Summer breeze.

While here and there is a vivid fleck,
   Wherever sunbeams can filter through,
On sloping shoulder and curving neck
   Of bay, or brown, or of chestnut hue.

And drowsing there, in the noon-day heat,
 Amidst the meadows they know so well,
They dream, perhaps, of the Opening Meet,
 Or mighty runs wherein blood will tell.

When these same fields may be wet and drear,
 And bare the trees from the wind's attack,
Then Winter wakes to the huntsman's cheer,
 And glorious cry of the flying pack.

~

[118]

DOROTHY WELLESLEY

FROM

Horses on the Fell

~

The horses stand on stormy skies
Hindquarters windward, like a thong
Their manes are lashed across their eyes;
On the streaked sunsets go headlong
The sounding splendour of their trails,
Before the dawns, light windy teams,
Winged stallions of the Nordic tales,
They are not horses, they are dreams.

For see! beneath storm buffeted stars
Their flanks are phosphorescent, then,
What Holy Twins, what Songs, what Wars
Possess them, through the sleep of men?

See! Taut with slashing tails unshorn
They wait in twilight, dappled, dun,

Till in the great white spate of dawn,
They are the Horses of the Sun.
They drink the fountains, leap on death,
Chimera, Hero-friends they know, –
Fiery and sacred is their breath,
And like the whirlwind they must go
While lasts the world, upon the heights.
Their hooves ring heavenward silver shod,
They strike the lightening, scattering lights,
This is the cavalcade of God.

≈

[119]

PETER CORNISH
Lady Midas

≈

Behold
My sovereign Lady
Crisp the guinea ground

Spendthrift branches
Scatter gold on gold

Paddock-bound
Under awnings riven
We (medallion pair
Sunstruck this Moulton morning)
Light-encircled seem
Alchemically given
One sole self to share

A centaur's dream
I know

Meanwhile
The gate hangs wide
With Jack beside

'Just see her go!'

We smile

O, now she is herself
Mine no more than flashing water
Dissolved in radiant air
Already in a wild half-circle
Gone plunging fifty yards
Head twisted down, towards her own truth

Her tail plumes
Her hoofs glitter

Unbridled, charged by joyous scorn
Spirit-swelled, she kicks away
Box,
Tack
School
Grooms
All our wickedness
All mishandlings since she was born

And I, forsworn
Find her
Lost to my manage
Lovely beyond telling
Transformed
Cresting some brilliant wave
That she alone can see
Up reaching

Mounted on some capricious cloud
Pegasus should serve
This divinity

Come
Close the gate

Tonight she will step down
Will kiss the carrot-furnished clown
Suffer me to cherish
Lead
Her gold to burnish
Feed
While still, untarnished
Her wealth will lie
Unguessed

Long since
My freedom perished.
I gave them best.
Collared, backed,
By work's long reign
Hacked, dispossessed,
Uncrowned
A prince of pain

But sovereign she

Come Jack
Now we to base turn back

Now we are stable bound.

≈

[120]

PHILIP LARKIN
At Grass
≈

The eye can hardly pick them out
From the cold shade they shelter in,
Till wind distresses tail and mane;

Then one crops grass, and moves about
– The other seeming to look on –
And stands anonymous again.

Yet fifteen years ago, perhaps
Two dozen distances sufficed
To fable them: faint afternoons
Of Cups and Stakes and Handicaps,
Whereby their names were artificed
To inlay faded, classic Junes –

Silks at the start: against the sky
Numbers and parasols: outside,
Squadrons of empty cars, and heat,
And littered grass: then the long cry
Hanging unhushed till it subside
To stop-press columns on the street.

Do memories plague their ears like flies?
They shake their heads. Dusk brims the shadows.
Summer by summer all stole away,
The starting-gates, the crowds and cries –
All but the unmolesting meadows.
Almanacked, their names live; they

Have slipped their names, and stand at ease,
Or gallop for what must be joy,
And not a fieldglass sees them home,
Or curious stop-watch prophesies:
Only the groom, and the groom's boy,
With bridles in the evening come.

~

[121]

TU FU

Ch'in Province

TRANSLATED BY
Richard King

~

Those who serve in the West need Heavenly Horses,
For some time they have been driven there in ten thousands.
Vast numbers perished in successive battles,
Autumn grass covers the mountain pastures.

I have heard that there were real dragon-steeds,
But those that are left look old and worn out.
Yet they still pine for the battle-fields,
Far away, they stand and gaze up at the expanse of blue.

~

EDRIC ROBERTS
Pensioned

~

With your mane bedraggled – once proudly plaited –
    And a tangled fore-lock across your brow,
With your coat unclipped and your tail all matted,
    You are pensioned off in the paddock now.

What a joy you were on a hunting morning,
    With your chestnut colour like burnished brass,
When you flicked your heels, as a playful warning,
    In the first mad gallop across the grass.

How you carved the way in those peerless Seasons –
    There was not a fence that you would not face –
And we led the Field, for the best of reasons
    That your heart was set in its proper place.

Happy days that, surely, you yet remember
    When you raise your gallant old head up high,
As the pack goes forth to a new November,
    And you stand entranced, till the echoes die.

~

W. K. HOLMES

The Old Brown Horse

~

The old brown horse looks over the fence
In a weary sort of way;
He seems to be saying to all who pass
'Well, folks, I've had my day –
I'm simply watching the world go by,
And nobody seems to mind,
As they're dashing past in their motor-cars
A horse who is lame and half-blind.'

The old brown horse has a shaggy coat,
But once he was young and trim,
And he used to trot through the woods and lanes
With the man who was fond of him.
But his master rides in a motor-car
And it makes him feel quite sad
When he thinks of the days that used to be,
And of all the times they had.

Sometimes a friendly soul will stop
Near the fence, where the tired old head
Rests wearily on the topmost bar,
And a friendly word is said.
Then the old brown horse gives a little sigh
As he feels the kindly touch
Of a hand on his mane, or his shaggy coat,
And he doesn't mind so much.

So if you pass the field one day,
Just stop for a word or two
With the old brown horse who was once as young
And as full of life as you.
He'll love the touch of your soft young hand,
And I know he'll seem to say –
'Oh, thank you, friend, for the kindly thought
For a horse who has had his day.'

~

[124]

JOHN ORR EWING
My Pal
~

He hears my step at the stable door,
The old horse whinnies, and paws the floor –
And if sweet apples are good to eat,
How else, indeed, can a dumb friend greet?

Does he remember the way they ran
The day they met at the old 'Green Man'?
When first flight fairy, nor thrusting gent
Could, none of them, follow the way he went?

The brook was wide, and its waters deep,
With crumbling banks where one had to leap,
'Twas bold might do it, but craven not –
He rocketed over, and cleared the lot!

And did hounds check on the farther shore?
No! On they ran for an hour, and more –
I have but pity, and deep regrets
For people who think that a horse forgets.

~

[125]

FELIX LEAKEY

What to Do with Old Hunting Gear
~

I wonder: 'Shall I ever use them again?'
                        My wife says:
'Throw them all *away*! For one thing,
We shan't have room for them in the new flat;
And anyway, good Heavens, you just haven't *time* to hunt!
And there's another thing: what about the risk of injury
To that precious brainbox of yours, upon which
Your whole way of life now depends?
Besides which (just to clinch matters),
Think how old and decrepit you're getting!'

She may well be right. But I don't know:
Life is full of surprises,
Isn't it? Maybe I'll just stow them away in a corner.
After all, even glancing at them, now and then
(Boots, hat, breeches, spurs, whip and tie, the whole lot),
Sets the old pulse racing away, just a bit . . .

~

W. B. YEATS

FROM

The Ballad of the Foxhunter

~

'To stable and to kennel go;
Bring what is there to bring;
Lead my Lollard to and fro,
Or gently in a ring.

'Put the chair upon the grass:
Bring Rody and his hounds,
That I may contented pass
From these earthly bounds.'

. . .

Brown Lollard treads upon the lawn,
And to the armchair goes,
And now the old man's dreams are gone,
He smooths the long brown nose.

~

[127]

G. J. WHYTE-MELVILLE

FROM

The Coal-Black Steed

~

His head! What a beautiful head he's got!
And his tail's put on in the proper spot;
While four such legs for muscle and bone,

You may travel a week and not be shown.
His mouth's so good; he's so easy to ride,
A child may safely be trusted to guide;
For when put out to his utmost speed,
A thread would pull up my coal-black steed.

. . .

When nature fails (and one day she will),
My gallant old horse I'll keep thee still;
In summer thy food and shelter shall be
The verdant mead and the leafy tree;
In winter a roomy shed, with law
To run in a yard well filled with straw;
And every night and morn a feed
Of corn will I give to my coal-black steed.

≈

[128]

TU FU

A Thin Horse

TRANSLATED BY
Richard King

≈

The thin horse in the Eastern Wasteland distresses me,
His bones stand out like pillars on a wall.
Hitched up, he tries to move, but staggers and keels over
Yet how he still longs to prance and step high!

If you examine the six brands, he bears the official stamp,
He was left at the roadside by the three armies.
His skin is dry and flaking, encrusted with mud,
His coat dull, he stands desolate in frost and snow.

Last year he strove in the chasing of the last bandits;
Hua-liu, unused to such treatment, could not have borne
     it.
Officers and men all use horses from the stables,
I am discouraged and fearful for him, the sickly Fei-
     huang.

Formerly he would spring over obstacles without a
     stumble;
Now he is rejected, there is no way you can protect him.
Seeing men he is grieved and feels an outcast,
Without a master he is confused, and his eyes are blurred.

In cold weather he is left to wander, with only geese for
     company.
In the evening he is not brought in, and crows peck his
     sores.
If someone were to care for him, he would be loyal,
Strive for him next year when the spring grass grows.

≈

[129]

WILLIAM BLAKE

FROM

Auguries of Innocence
≈

A dog starv'd at his Master's Gate
Predicts the ruin of the State.
A Horse misus'd upon the Road
Calls to Heaven for Human blood.

≈

CHARLES DIBDIN
The High-Mettled Racer

~

See the course throng'd with gazers, the sports are begun,
Confusion but hear, I bet you sir, done:
Ten thousand strange murmurs resound far and near,
Lords, hawkers, and jockies, assail the tir'd ear;
While with neck like a rainbow erecting his crest,
Pamper'd, prancing, and pleas'd, his head touching his
            breast,
Scarcely snuffing the air, he's so proud and elate,
The high-mettled Racer first starts for the plate.

Now Reynard's turn'd out, and o'er hedge and ditch rush,
Dogs, horses, and huntsmen, all hard at his brush;
Thro' marsh, fen, and brier, led by their sly prey,
They by scent, and by view, chace a long tedious way;
While alike born for sports of the field and the course,
Always sure to come through – a stanch and fleet horse;
When fairly run down, the Fox yields up his breath,
The high-mettled Racer is in at the death.

Grown aged, us'd up, and turn'd out of the stud,
Lame, spavin'd, and wind-gall'd, but yet with some blood,
While knowing postillions his pedigree trace,
Tell his dame won this sweep, his sire won that race,
And what matches he won to the hostlers count o'er,
As they loiter their time at some hedge-ale-house door,
While the harness sore galls, and the spurs his sides goad,
The high-mettled Racer's a hack on the road.

Till at last having labour'd, dragg'd early and late,
Bow'd down by degrees he bends on to his fate,
Blind, old, lean, and feeble, he tugs round a mill,
Or draws sand, till the sand of his hourglass stands still;
And now cold and lifeless, expos'd to the view,
In the very same cart that he yesterday drew,
While a pitying crowd his sad relics surrounds,
The high-mettled Racer is sold for the hounds.

❦

[131]

EDRIC ROBERTS
The Old 'Un
❦

I am not as young as I used to be,
    But I feel the thrill of it, just the same,
With the cry of hounds, and the ecstasy
    Of the rush of hoofs in the greatest game.

I am not as fast as I used to be,
    But can hold my own, when the going's deep,
And I know the country like A.B.C.,
    And I'll get you there, if I crawl and creep.

I am not the 'looker' I used to be,
    But I'm none the worse for a few old scars,
And I'm not ashamed of a blemished knee,
    If I rap the wall or the timber-bars.

I am not as sound as I used to be,
    And I 'make a noise', it is true, no doubt,
And I 'dot and carry' for all to see,
    But it matters not, if my heart is stout.

I am not the stylist I used to be,
    But I'll get you out of an awkward place,
And I'll never fall, I can guarantee,
    If you let me go at my own set pace.

I am not as young as I used to be,
    I shall soon have done my appointed task,
But I trust the fates will be kind to me,
    And 'to die in harness' is all I ask.

~

[132]

A. B. PATERSON

FROM

Old Pardon, the Son of Reprieve

~

But he's old – and his eyes are grown hollow;
    Like me, with my thatch of the snow;
When he dies, then I hope I may follow,
    And go where the racehorses go,
I don't want no harping nor singing –
    Such things with my style don't agree;

Where the hoofs of the horses are ringing
   There's music sufficient for me.

And surely the thoroughbred horses
   Will rise up again and begin
Fresh races on far-away courses,
   And p'raps they might let me slip in.
It would look rather well the race-card on
   'Mongst Cherubs and Seraphs and things,
'Angel Harrison's black gelding Pardon,
   Blue halo, white body and wings.'

And if they have racing hereafter,
   (And who is to say they will not?)
When the cheers and the shouting and laughter
   Proclaim that the battle grows hot;
As they come down the racecourse a-steering,
   He'll rush to the front, I believe;
And you'll hear the great multitude cheering
   For Pardon, the son of Reprieve.

~

[133]

ANONYMOUS

The Little Worn-Out Pony

~

There's a little worn-out pony this side of Hogan's shack
With a snip upon his nuzzle and a mark upon his back;
Just a common little pony is what most people say,
But then of course they've never heard what happened in
       his day:
I was droving on the Leichhardt with a mob of pikers wild,
When this tibby little pony belonged to Hogan's child.

One night it started raining – we were camping on a rise,
When the wind blew cold and bleakly and thunder shook
      the skies;
The lightning cut the figure eight around the startled
      cattle,
Then down there fell torrential rains and then began a
      battle.
In a fraction of an instant the wild mob became insane,
Careering through the timber helter-skelter for the plain.

The timber fell before them like grass before a scythe,
And heavy rain in torrents poured from the grimly
      blackened sky;
The mob rushed ever onward through the slippery sodden
      ground,
While the men and I worked frantically to veer their
      heads around;
And then arose an awful cry – it came from Jimmy Rild,
For there between two saplings straight ahead was
      Hogan's child.

I owned not man or devil, I had not prayed since when,
But I called upon the blessed Lord to show His mercy
then;
I shut my eyes and ground my teeth, the end I dared not
see
Great God! The cattle – a thousand head – were crashing
through the trees.
'God pity us bush children in our darkest hour of need,'
Were the words I prayed although I followed neither
church nor creed.

Then my right-hand man was shouting, the faithful
Jimmy Rild,
'Did you see it, Harry, see the way he saved that child?'
'Saved! Saved, did you say?' and I shot upright with a
bound,
'Yes, saved,' he said, 'indeed old man, the child is safe
and sound.
I was feeling pretty shaky and was gazing up the track,
Just then a pony galloped, the kid hopped on its back.

'A blinding flash of lightning then the thunder's rolling
crack;
With two hands clasped upon his mane he raced towards
the shack.'
'Good heavens, man,' I shouted then, 'if that is truly so,
To blazes with the cattle, to the shanty we must go.'
We reached Bill Hogan's shanty in fifteen minutes' ride,
Then left our horses standing and wildly rushed inside.
The little child was there unhurt but shivering with fear,
And Hogan told us, 'Yes, thank God, there's the pony
brought her here.'

There's a little worn-out pony just this side of Hogan's
shack
With a snip upon his nuzzle and a mark upon his back.
Just a common little pony is what most people say,
But I doubt if there's his equal in the pony world today.

~

WILL H. OGILVIE

The Battered Brigade

~

The mark of a stake in the shoulder,
　The brand of a wall on the knee,
Are scars to the careless beholder
　And blemishes. So it may be;
But every such blemish endorses
　The pluck of a steed unafraid,
And the heart of a lover of horses
　Goes out to the Battered Brigade.

Their knocks have been gathered in duty,
　Their scars in the front of the fray;
It isn't your cleanest-legged beauty
　That's first at the end of the day.
When five foot of timber before us
　Has half of the pretty ones stayed,
If you want to catch up to the chorus
　Come on with the Battered Brigade!

~

EDRIC ROBERTS

FROM

The Hireling

~

I wonder what his story is
And why he should be living
This unromantic life of his,
With all its vague uncertainties
Which fill one with misgiving.

For, by his looks, he ought to grace
Some private stable, plainly;
He seems to have a turn of pace
And might, perhaps, pick up a race,
If treated more humanely.

But every hunting day, instead,
He's out, or very nearly,
With someone pulling at his head,
Or bumping like a lump of lead
About his saddle, queerly.

It rarely seems to be his lot
To carry good performers,
Or even ones who know a jot
About the things to do, or not,
Out hunting, as conformers.

~

TU FU

A Sick Horse

TRANSLATED BY
Richard King

~

I have ridden you a long time now,
Beneath cold skies in remote border regions.
You have aged and weakened in the dust of travel
In your last years, your sickness grieves me.

Your hair and bones do not differ from another's
But you have always been loyal up to now.
Though a mere animal, your spirit is not shallow,
I am moved by this, and heave a long sigh.

~

P. G. R. BENSON

The Knacker Horses
~

Horses that stand in the field
    Close by the hound Kennel yard,
Ponies from moorland and weald,
    Broken and aged and scarred!

Hunters that once in their pride
    Champed at a glittering bit,

Taking a brook in their stride,
  Ponies that worked in the pit,

Draught-horse that once in his prime
  Dragged heavy cannon to war,
Spurning the stress of the climb,
  Weary and wasted and sore!

Gunner that leapt in the trace
  Touched by the whip on his crest,
Proud in his strength and his pace,
  Finished and longing for rest!

Horses that ploughed on the land,
  Patiently plodding along,
Praised by caress of the hand,
  Heartened by lark's merry song,

Where is the voice of the bird?
  Where is the smell of the lay?
Where is the welcoming word?
  Where the reward of the day?

Victims of battle and strife!
    Relics of work and of war!
Flotsam and jetsam of life,
    Wreckage washed up on the shore!

Now that your labour is done
    Soon shall your suffering cease,
Soon shall your guerdon be won –
    Freedom from pain, and God's peace!

~

[138]

ANONYMOUS

With Apologies to Gray

~

Full many a horse of purest blood, I ween
Of man's blind ignorance must bear the stab;
Full many a racer has to blush unseen
Between the blinkers, in a London cab.

Some Isinglass that once with matchless speed
Might well have heard victorious shouts of joy
Is deemed by ignorance a worthless weed,
And gallops round the Row a lady's toy.

Far from the madding crowd's more noble strife
His sober wishes never learned to stray,
But round the ring of fashionable life
He keeps the even canter of his way.

The thoughtless world to victory may bow,
Exalt the winner, idolise success;

But in these precincts I would wander now
To those whom fortune ne'er conspired to bless.

And I, who mindful of the unhonoured dead,
Do in these notes their woeful lot relate,
Am by this spot's associations led
To meditate thus sadly on their fate.

~

[139]

LLYWELYN LUCAS
The Dustman's Horse
~

Dappled and silver-white,
With a mane
Like drifting smoke . . .
Plumes of a proud design
Of kingly mountain line

That crafty Mankind broke . . .
The old horse stands and dreams,
And shakes his dusty mane
Free, like a withered rain
Of all things noble, spent.

Dreams of a sire of brumbies,
Colts and mares,
Out on the hills,
With the wind in their ruddy nostrils,
Their windy hearts full of the lifting fires
Of the mountain folks' affairs!
Mountains for mountain people!

Glimmering hooves,
And the suppleness of the limb attuned to fear,
Making it bright with its daring!
Hands of the clouds on the hills,

Soft as a spirit singing
Its ageless, muttered rune
Where murmuring Nature tells
Of the mysteries of Time,
And the magpies strongly winging,
Carols a mighty tune
Like innumerable bells,
And as simple and sublime!
Mountains for mountain folk!

The old grey leader spoke,
And his mane was as driven smoke,
And his hide was the colour of milk,
With the dapples in the grain
Like misted mountain-rain
Spun with a shaft of silk.

Flashing and flighty,
Fillies, taut as wire,
Untutored by the tendance, yet, of foals,
Listen, half-dreaming, to the old grey sire
(Whose end will come in one age-shaken breath
Upon a crag . . . leaping like some old sun
To shake the mountains in its death).

. . . The gallops of the mob!
The wheel! The rush!
The flying withers pressing in the crush!
Warmth, pasture, freedom, madness, merriment!
The foam upon the flank of bay and black,
The thudding on resilience of grass,
The scream of bitten things,
And all the rhythmic tide
Of Nature free!

II

(But free no more – alas!
. . . The carter's children now upon him ride!
No gold-eyed mare will call a dappled stallion back!)

He dreams . . . the old, grey sire,
Long, grey-white dreams,
That rise like mountain fire!
Mankind has tamed the wild,
Broken it, and defiled;
Mankind has tamed mankind;
And, atrophied and blind,
Shuffles with sleepy feet
About a dirty street.

'Let us be rich!' he cries,
'Let us be free, and wise!'
– Who once had splendid health
Of mind and muscle-wealth!
– Who once was kinsman free
To cataract and tree!
And knowledge had beyond
The bloody blade, or bond.

Clod hoof! . . . Clod heart! . . . Clod . . . clod!
Finished the strife of wills,
Lost the enscarped hills,
And gone the mountain god.

~

ADAM LINDSAY GORDON

Hippodromania
Banker's Dream

~

Of chases and courses dogs dream, so do horses –
   Last night I was dozing and dreaming,
The crowd and the bustle were there, and the rustle
   Of the silk in the autumn sky gleaming.

The stand throng'd with faces, the broadcloth and laces,
   The booths, and the tents, and the cars,
The bookmakers' jargon, for odds making bargain,
   The nasty stale smell of cigars.

We formed into line, 'neath the merry sunshine,
   Near the logs at the end of the railing;
'Are you ready, boys? Go!' cried the starter, and low
   Sank the flag, and away we went sailing.

In the van of the battle we heard the stones rattle,
   Some slogging was done, but no slaughter,
A shout from the stand, and the whole of our band
   Skimm'd merrily over the water.

Two fences we clear'd, and the roadway we near'd,
   When three of our troop came to trouble;
Like a bird on the wing, or a stone from a sling,
   Flew Cadger, first over the double.

And Western was there, head and tail in the air,
   And Pondon was there, too – what noodle
Could so name a horse? I should feel some remorse
   If I gave such a name to a poodle.

In and out of the lane, to the racecourse again,
 Craig's pony was first, I was third,
And Ingleside lit in my tracks, with the bit
 In his teeth, and came up 'like a bird'.

In the van of the battle we heard the rails rattle,
 Says he, 'Though I don't care for shunning
My share of the raps, I shall look out for gaps,
 When the light weight's away with the running.'

At the fence just ahead, the outsider still led,
 The chestnut play'd follow my leader,
Oh! the devil! a gap, he went into it slap,
 And he and his jock took a header.

Says Ingleside, 'Mate, should the pony go straight,
 You've no time to stop or turn restive';
Says I, 'Who means to stop? I shall go till I drop';
 Says he, 'Go it, old cuss, gay and festive.'

The fence stiff and tall, just beyond the log wall,
 We cross'd, and the walls, and the water, –
I took off too near, a small made fence to clear,
 And just touch'd the grass with my snorter.

At the next post and rail up went Western's bang tail,
 And down (by the very same token)
To earth went his nose, for the panel he chose
 Stood firm and refused to be broken.

I dreamt some one said that the bay would have made
 The race safe, if he'd *stood* a while longer;
If he had – but, like if, there the panel stands stiff –
 He stood, but the panel stood stronger.

In and out of the road, with a clear lead still show'd
 The violet fluted with amber;
Says Johnson, 'Old man, catch him now if you can;
 'Tis the second time round, you'll remember.'

At the road once again, pulling hard on the rein,
    Craig's pony popp'd in and popp'd out;
I followed like smoke, and the pace was no joke,
    For his friends were beginning to shout.

And Ingleside came to my side, strong and game,
    And once he appeared to outstrip me,
But I felt the steel gore, and I shot to the fore,
    Only Cadger seem'd likely to whip me.

In the van of the battle I heard the logs rattle,
    His stroke never seem'd to diminish,
And thrice I drew near him, and thrice he drew clear,
    For the weight served him well at the finish.

Ha! Cadger goes down, see, he stands on his crown –
    Those rails take a power of clouting –
A long sliding blunder – he's up – well, I wonder
    If now it's all over but shouting.

All loosely he's striding, the amateur's riding
    All loosely, some reverie lock'd in
Of a 'vision in smoke', or a 'wayfaring bloke',
    His poetical rubbish concocting.

Now comes from afar the faint cry, 'Here they are',
    'The violet winning with ease',
'Fred goes up like a shot', 'Does he catch him or not?'
    'Level money, I'll take the cerise.'

To his haunches I spring, and my muscle I bring
    To his flank, to his girth, to his shoulder;
Through the shouting and yelling I hear my name swelling,
    The hearts of my backers grow bolder.

Neck and neck! head and head! staring eye! nostril spread!
    Girth and stifle laid close to the ground!
Stride for stride! stroke for stroke! through one hurdle we've
            broke!
    On the splinters we've lit with one bound.

And 'Banker for choice' is the cry, and one voice
   Screams, 'Six to four once upon Banker';
'Banker wins', 'Banker's beat', 'Cadger wins', 'A dead heat' –
   'Ah! there goes Fred's whalebone a flanker.'

Springs the whip with a crack! nine stone ten on his back,
   Fit and light he can race like the devil;
I draw past him – 'tis vain; he draws past me again,
   Springs the whip! and again we are level.

Steel and cord do their worst, now my head struggles first!
   That tug my last spurt has expended –
Nose to nose! lip to lip! from the sound of the whip
   He strains to the utmost extended.

How they swim through the air, as we roll to the chair,
   Stand, faces, and railings flit past;
Now I spring * * *
               from my lair, with a snort and a stare,
Rous'd by Fred with my supper at last.

~

[141]

JOHN ORR EWING

Olympia, 1932
Parade of the National Winners

~

Eight of the best that ever looked through bridle!
A very gallant company are these.
None have more surely won the right to idle
In fields Elysian, and take their ease.

Do they recall the thrill when they were nearing
The hard-won goal on their red-letter day?
Can they yet hear an echo of the cheering
That greeted them from Aintree's dense array?

They do not seem so very proud about it.
They've dignity, these gentlemen of note.
Did people watch, whose eyes were dry? I doubt it.
I know I had a big lump in my throat.

~

[142]

MARY VAUGHAN
Red Rum
~

It's said there are horses for courses,
Red Rum makes this point very clear;
Three *firsts* and a couple of seconds –
His astonishing Aintree career!

Forbidding, formidable fences
Four miles and a half of the track;
Red Rum, all alert in his senses,
Is in tune with the man on his back.

Around forty magnificent chasers
Well prepared by their trainers' skilled art
For this greatest of all steeplechases
Fit and ready and rearing to start.

'They are off' with high hearts and high courage;
'Every horse has the National won!'
But few there will be at the finish
For there's gruelling work to be done.

His wonderful galloping quarters
Land him easily over The Chair;
Spring-heeled and well balanced at Becher's
He flies like a bird through the air.

While his rivals are falling about him
He cocks an intelligent ear,
He knows he must keep out of trouble
And there's plenty of that around here.

The last fence, and then the long run in,
Sustained by his courage alone,
Till he hears the crowd roaring for 'Rummy'
And knows he's triumphantly home.

And now he is feted and honoured
Befitting so gallant a horse.
His statue at Aintree proclaims him
King of the National Course.

~

[143]

R. S. SURTEES

FROM

Mr Sponge's Sporting Tour
~

There is no secret so close as that between
a rider and his horse.

~

JOHN ORR EWING
Brown Jack

~

Who is as staunch as he is fleet?
Who never knows when he is beat?
Why, everybody knows his name –
'Brown Jack'!

And who are they that share with him
The honours of the struggle grim?
'Tis 'Come on, Steve!', who holds the reins,
And Ivor Anthony, who trains
'Brown Jack'.

Amid the thunder of the cheers
Not many eyes are far from tears,
And throats without a lump are few,
For hearts are deeply stirred by you,
'Brown Jack'!

~

JOHN MASEFIELD
FROM
Right Royal

~

It was the strangest dream I ever had.
. . .
     And I looked, and, lo!
There was Right Royal, speaking, at my side.

The horse's very self, and yet his hide
Was like, what shall I say? like pearl on fire,
A white soft glow of burning that did twire
Like soft white-heat with every breath he drew.
A glow, with utter brightness running through;
Most splendid, though I cannot make you see.

His great crest glittered as he looked at me
Criniered with spitting sparks; he stamped the ground
All crock and fire, trembling like a hound,
And glad of me, and eager to declare
His horse's mind.
                                And I was made aware
That, being a horse, his mind could only say
Few things to me. He said, 'It is my day,
My day, today; I shall not have another.'

And as he spoke he seemed a younger brother
Most near, and yet a horse, and then he grinned
And tossed his crest and crinier to the wind,
And looked down to the Water with an eye
All fire of soul to gallop dreadfully.

. . .

As he knotted the reins and took his stand
The horse's soul came into his hand,
And up from the mouth that held the steel
Came an innermost word, half thought, half feel,
'My day today, O master, O master;
None shall jump cleaner, none shall go faster,
Call till you kill me, for I'll obey,
It's my day today, it's my day today.'

In a second more he had found his seat,
And the standers-by jumped clear of feet,
For the big dark bay all fire and fettle
Had his blood in a dance to show his mettle.

~

ROBERT DODSLEY
The Racehorse
~

Easy in motion, perfect in his form,
His boasted lineage drawn from steeds of blood,
He the fleet courser, too, exulting shows
And points with pride his beauties. Neatly set
His lively head, and glowing in his eye
True spirit lives. His nostril wide inhales
With ease the ambient air. His body firm
And round, upright his joints, his horny hoof
Small, shining light, and large his ample reach.
His limbs, though slender, braced with sinewy strength,
Declare his winged speed. His temper mild,
Yet high his mettled heart. Hence in the race,
All emulous, he hears the clashing whips,
He feels the animating shouts; exerts
With eagerness his utmost powers; and strains,
And springs, and flies, to reach the destin'd goal.

~

[147]

JOHN MASEFIELD
The Racer
~

I saw the racer coming to the jump,
Staring with fiery eyeballs as he rushed,
I heard the blood within his body thump,
I saw him launch, I heard the toppings crushed.

And as he landed I beheld his soul
Kindle, because, in front, he saw the Straight
With all its thousands roaring at the goal,
He laughed, he took the moment for his mate.

Would that the passionate moods on which we ride
Might kindle thus to oneness with the will;
Would we might see the end to which we stride,
And feel, not strain, in struggle, only thrill.

And laugh like him and know in all our nerves
Beauty, the spirit, scattering dust and turves.

~

[148]

HOMER
~

At once the coursers from the barrier bound;
The lifted scourges all at once resound;
Loose on their shoulders the long manes reclined
Float in their speed, and dance upon the wind.

~

[149]

BRYAN WALLER PROCTER

FROM

The Blood Horse

~

Gamarra is a noble steed;
Strong, black, and of the desert breed;
Full of fire, and full of bone,
All his line of fathers known;
Fine his nose, his nostrils thin,
But blown abroad by the pride within!
His mane, a stormy river flowing;
And his eyes, like embers glowing
In the darkness of the night;
And his pace as swift as light.

~

SIR ALAN HERBERT

FROM

Derby Day

~

Look at that horse! Must such a beauty die
To let more motor-bicycles rush by?
Go to your Parliament and search the crowd
For brows so thoughtful and an eye so proud!
Alas, we cannot without a dealer's art
Pick out his points and duly praise each part
(We know the horse as little as the car
And are not certain what the withers are),
But he indeed must have a flint for soul
Who without reverence regards the whole.
What fairy step! – that drop of Arab blood,
Sahara's tribute to the English stud!
Brave as a lion and as hard to kill,
He can stand anything but standing still.
He is on wires, suspended from the skies,
He is elastic – it would not surprise
If on a sudden he took wings and *flew*
Over the Downs and off to Timbuktu.

~

ALEXANDER POPE

FROM

The Fifth Satire

~

Then peers grew proud in horsemanship to excel,
Newmarket's glory rose, as Britain fell.

~

[152]

OLWEN WAY

Newmarket in June

~

Wind on the Heath
Tousles the grass
Tangs tails,
Slants manes
Waywardly,
Up on the Heath.

Colours matt
In the sandy dust
And no edge glints
To the eye
The tranquil duty
Of a summer day.

Yet right in focus
Somewhere

Racing June
Brewing her potion
Sits, tight-reined
Wide awake
Touting the technicolours
Of emotion.

~

ROBIN IVY

Autumn Gale

~

All along the road to the paddock
Under the blue silk of an Autumn sky,
Truncated limbs lie silver and grey,
Uprooted and tangled,
Twisted, flung in a ditch
Or crashed down on the carriageway.

The gale roared through the wood
Like shouts from the stands
When hard-driven horses
Strain for the winning-post.

Famous names,
Turned summer ghosts
After taking their chance
At landing the odds,
Have been stabled for winter
Or put out to stud.

For Dawn Run and Dancing Brave
The rails are dumb

Where strong men wept
At bold performances.

A saw rasps, an axe snaps,
To the crack and crackle of branches;
Tang of raw wood and sap
As bodies are chained
And eased on to trailers.

Shadowy figures light new pyres,
Call a greeting through drifting smoke
As they shuffle through golden leaves;
Treading on ashes
Of burnt-out memories
Before rides are green again
And hooves cut new turf
At the next Spring Meeting.

~

[154]

W. H. OGILVIE

FROM

Steeplechasers
~

Tucked away in winter quarters,
Gainsborough's sons and Buchan's daughters,
Blue of blood, clean-lined and handsome,
Priced beyond a prince's ransom,
Where no danger can befall them
Rest till next year's Classics call them;
And the limber lean-of-head ones,
Hardy, hefty, humble-bred ones,

Booted, bandaged to the knee,
Ready for whate'er may be,
Gallant slaves and cheery martyrs,
Stand once more before the starters.

. . .

So they forge through wind and weather
To the crack of straining leather
Lashing at the leaps together,
With the fluttering flags to guide them,
Taking what the Fates provide them,
Danger calling, Death beside them. –
'Tis a game beyond gainsaying
Made by gods for brave men's playing.

~

ALISON BRACKENBURY
Cheltenham Races
~

It is a cold business. I have seen horses, under
The headlong rain, sprawled on its wet ground, lying
With leg or back past help; no longer trying
To rise: one ear pressed in the torn grass
Till the gun's shout. Are we then, kinder
To people? the small men in wheelchairs
Spin aside to watch the horses pass,
Still pale, alert and shrunk, they were once jockeys.

Quick winnings – yesterday's – a night's wild poker
Warm Irish travellers in slow ticket queues.

Remote and blue, cigar smoke licks round us.
Upon the skyline's hill a new warmth blows
From twigs where dark buds thicken and thrust higher.
Heads dip, quick waves of light above the crowd:
The horses. A white tail glints, it flows
In the parade ring's air. A silvered braid

Twists through the severe plaits of the girl
Who leads her hard-legged bay. He halts, the best:
But I watch the light grey: as all the rest
Bound on the bit to start, he turns to stare
Up in the humming sky which bends on him.
All curve through my binoculars, slow whirl
Of silks and backs, becoming something else:
The grey comes out of line, brushing through hurdles,
Eyes staring, pulling, pounding, into darkness –

A huge elbow rears up: it fills my sight –
They flicker back with light on the long hill.
The grey lags, now, the bay swings smoothly, will
Lead at the turn. Then I lose the last fence,
With forests of hats, hoarse shouting – Who is down?
Grey neighbour rips his ticket. The winners slow, they jog
Riders raise muddy goggles stare back:

he is still lying,

The great bay. There they stand
Ambulance men, a jockey, his thin girl
Who led him round – As we stand: quiet: he stirs,
Heaves to his feet, then shakes. At once, we cheer
Shuffle torn tickets, seeing the scarlet rug
Smoothed along his back – He walks through us
Slowly to stables; down the littered slope
Watched, warm as winner, led still by the silver,
Which glints in a girl's hair: old folly, hope.

~

[156]

SIEGFRIED SASSOON
What the Captain Said at the Point-to-Point

~

I've had a good bump round; my little horse
Refused the brook first time,
Then jumped it prime;
And ran out at the double,
But of course
There's always trouble at a double:
And then – I don't know how
It was – he turned it up
At that big, hair fence before the plough;
And some young silly pup
(I don't know which),
Near as a toucher knocked me into the ditch;
But we finished full of running, and quite sound:
And anyhow I've had a good bump round.

~

[157]

GLENDA SPOONER
Belinda

~

The smokey old lantern that hung on a nail
In the stone-cobbled yard of the Inn in the Vale,
Sputtered and spat as the wind-driven rain

Forced its way in through the cracks in the pane.
Curses and hissings, the whisking of tails –
Splashing of water, the clatter of pails;
    Medley of voices, the stamp of a hoof;
    White pigeons bickering up on the roof;
Sweet scent of hay, and when at last they appear
Whiffs of tobacco, the stench of stale beer
    And smell of wet tweed from a tough-looking crew
    Arrived from the 'pub' in the village to view
In her stable, the game little varminty bay
That everyone knew was a star in her day.

    Says one of the bunch – 'Dammit John, you're a chump
    To run her at all. Though we know she can jump
The mare isn't fit – it's a lamb to the slaughter –
She's never looked worse since the morning you bought her.'
    But all Johnny says is 'I may be a clown,
    But I tell you that mare's never yet let me down:
A bob to a button it'll be to your sorrow
If you don't put your shirts on Belinda tomorrow.'

    The race morning dawns with a mellowing light;
    The road to the course is a wonderful sight;
Charabanc, wagonette, lorry and bus
Missing its gears in the crush and the fuss;
    Fat bookies bulging out over their Ford
    Young men on bikes with their sweethearts on board;
Men selling race cards and offering slips
On which they have scribbled their dubious tips.
    Women and children, a babe in a pram
    Farmers on cobs – and, mixed up with the jam
On the road – unperturbed by the crowd, walked the bay
That everyone knew was a star in her day.

    A bell rang and cantering down to the start
    Admired by the crowd went the favourite 'Bold Heart'.
A big chestnut gelding who in Ireland had won
All six open races in which he had run.
    The 'Blue Bird' – a grey and the devil to sit

With back up and head down, he yawed at his bit.
'Mary Machree', 'Dunnimore', and 'Good Sport',
The first in a lather and the third striding short;
    And last of the bunch, not turning a hair
    Came John on Belinda, the little bay mare.

The white signal dropped – the Irish horse plunged,
The brown mare got left, and the grey gelding lunged;
    But Belinda jumped off and got into her stride
    As Johnny stood up in his irons to ride.
At the very first fence where Dunnimore fell
The grey and the chestnut were both jumping well;
    Two flights of rails saw the whole field across,
    But the big blackthorn did for a good 'local' horse.
With 'Bold Heart', the grey, and the bay safely over,
The fence a mile out – with the drop into clover –
    Stopped 'Mary Machree', and caused other trouble
    While 'Sport', who is cunning, ran out at the double.
Three fell in a heap at the 'open', but now
Though the going is deep coming over the plough
    The 'Blue Bird's' moved up to the favourite's side
    Till they're galloping level and stride for stride,
While, tucked in behind them not two lengths away
Is John on Belinda, the game little bay.

    They're hidden from view by a covert until
    They straddle the rise of the sun-freckled hill,
Then slip down the slope to the valley below
Where the menacing waters of Purley Brook flow.

    There the Irish horse leads by a good length or more –
    There's breathless hush. Then a deafening roar.
'My God, he's refused, and the grey horse is in –
If Johnny's not baulked, the bay mare can win.
    There, he's done it – by gad sir, hurrah for the mare
    I swear that she cleared it with inches to spare.'

Thereafter Belinda, with both her ears pricked,
Stayed on past the post to have them all licked.

A few mornings after, they opened her door
  To discover Belinda stretched out on her straw,
And lying beside her – why, God bless my soul,
Was a right little, tight little, bay filly foal.

≈

[158]

JOSEPH HALL

On the Importance of the Dam
≈

Say'st thou this colt shall prove a swift paced steed
Only because a jennet did him breed,
Or say'st thou this same horse shall win the prize
Because his dam was swiftest Tranchefice?

≈

[159]

W. B. YEATS

At Galway Races
≈

There where the course is,
Delight makes all of the one mind,
The riders upon the galloping horses,

The crowd that closes in behind:
We, too, had good attendance once,
Hearers and hearteners of the work;
Aye, horsemen for companions,
Before the merchant and the clerk
Breathed on the world with timid breath.
Sing on: somewhere at some new moon,
We'll learn that sleeping is not death,
Hearing the whole earth change its tune,
Its flesh being wild, and it again
Crying aloud as the racecourse is,
And we find hearteners among men
That ride upon horses.

~

[160]

JOHN MASEFIELD
An Epilogue
~

I have seen flowers come in stony places
And kind things done by men with ugly faces,
And the gold cup won by the worst horse at the races,
So I trust, too.

~

ALAN ROSS
The Starter

~

'They're off!'
              and the fat major,
C.O. of the start, returns on his nag,
Sagging and bellying on the journey back,
To wet his moustache in a flapping tent,
Sweat running off him in moist content.

              And away on the first circuit –
As through myopic eyes, crunching a water-biscuit,
He gazes at clouds sailing with manes
Fleecily white – taking the bit as, prancing,
They clear the long line of the Downs, the horses bunch
              and jump,
Brushing the hurdles, pause, then thump
To safety, lengthening their stride
By the railway, and, turned for the straight,
Aim at the Downs, Stands on their off-side.

The leaders string out, detaching
Their colours like threads being pulled
From a pattern, one under
Pressure, one coming late in a clap of thunder,
One jumping wide – their breaths
Pluming and heavy, lather
On their flanks, and one tubed one wheezy as death –
A flail of hooves, flying through grass and clover,

And it's over –
              The patterns re-form
Round bookmakers, bars and paddocks,
A ballet of profit and loss, as tension
Subsides and pulses descend to normal.
'Weighed in', and already preparations begin

For the next race, tick-tack telegraphs
Busily at work, the graphs
On the Tote rehearsing the punter.

And the little men, knowing
As Cabinet Ministers, presiding in the Ring
With owners anxious as parents at parents' meetings.
                    And soon the Starter, hiccoughing
Gently, heaves himself up, adjusting
His stirrup and his own girth, and canters,
Black-bowlered and rakish, on his rocking-horse,
              Back to the start.

≈

[162]

ANONYMOUS

Epsom
A Satire 1828

≈

High on the downs the awful ring is made,
The gath'ring clan of all the blackleg trade;
A thousand shouts increase the deaf'ning cry,
And quite confound all questions and reply;
Yet order still o'er madness holds her rule,
And Cocker's self might learn in Gulley's school.
The storm increases, swell the pencill'd score;
And lords and senators and bullies roar.
The statelier crew, their speculation made,
Forsake the rabble, and invest the glade;
Where, just led out, the paragons are seen
To press, not wound, with glitt'ring hoof the green.
Each arching neck's impatient of the rein,
Fire in each eye, and swelling ev'ry vein.

Back to a hundred sires of Arab breed
Trace we the bottom and enquire the speed;
By Selim this, and that by Phantom got;
And this by Tramp was bred by Mr Watt.
And memory now in praise is fond to trace
Friends of the turf and patrons of the race;
Smolensko, last of skilful Bunbury's breed,
Whom Jersey's Earl and Grafton's Duke succeed;
Their care, their hope, their profit and their pride
A moment may o'erturn, and must decide.
That moment comes, – the bell! the saddling bell,
Sounds fortune's proudest triumph or her knell!
How beats our hero's pulse? or where his heart? –
They're off! but order'd back for a false start.
They're ranged again! and now are off! – I deem
Two minutes now two lagging ages seem;
Till twice ten thousand shouts and yells proclaim,
That Jersey's Marmeluke wins deathless fame.
Some weep for joy, some think 'twas falsely done,
And swear Glenartney might with ease have won.

~

[163]

WILLIAM SHAKESPEARE

FROM

King Henry V
Prologue

~

Think, when we talk of horses, that you see them
Printing their proud hoofs i' the receiving earth.

~

SIR FRANCIS HASTINGS DOYLE

FROM

The Doncaster St Leger 1827

~

He's sixth – he's fifth – he's fourth – he's third,
And on, like some glancing meteor-flame
The stride of the Derby winner came . . .
One other bound – once more – 'tis done;
Right up to her the horse has run,
And head to head and stride for stride,
Newmarket's hope and Yorkshire's pride.
Like horses harnessed side by side
Are struggling to the goal . . .
He's beat! he's beat! – by heaven the mare!
Just on the post, her spirit rare,
When Hope herself might well despair;
When Time had not a breath to spare;
With bird-like dash shoots clean away,
And by half a length has gained the day.

~

G. A. FOTHERGILL
'Danny' Maher's Dead Heat

Recalling the famous jockey's own thoughts during the historic
finish of the Eclipse Stakes (£10,000), when he on Lord Rosebery's
Neil Gow dead-heated with Mr Fairie's Lemberg. (A short while
before, the same two horses, with the same jockeys up (Dillon rode
Lemberg), met in the 2000 Guineas, and Neil Gow won by a short
head.) Maher had said he was 'desperately anxious to win for the
greatest sportsman in the land, Lord Rosebery'. He was riding, he
said, 'the funniest horse that any man could ever ride, one which
you know can win *if* he cares to'.

~

Two furlongs from home he draws up to the horse,
The *only* one left to beat on the course.
What a maddening anxiety! (to others sublime) –
What a strain crowded into some seconds of time!
'Danny' feels he is hanging, not doing his best –
  Ah! here is the rub – must he still hesitate
To hit him in dread of his *then* doing less? –
  Must he be but a slug? – is it all but too late? –
He had desperately ridden him with hands and with
        heels –
He had made to his senses the best of appeals;
So he picks up the whip to just risk it,
Gives him one light'ning cut on the brisket, –
And now comes the grief that he's lost him the race
As he swerves from the whip – no, he puts on the pace,
In a whirl of excitement they're just past the post,
Head and head, to know who has won and who's lost . . .
A dead heat! – even that is relief to his ears,
And he welcomes the verdict 'midst deafening cheers.

~

ADAM LINDSAY GORDON

How We Beat the Favourite
A Lay of the Loamshire Hunt Cup

~

'Aye, squire,' said Stevens, 'they back him at evens;
　The race is all over, bar shouting, they say;
The Clown ought to beat her; Dick Neville is sweeter
　Than ever – he swears he can win all the way.

'A gentleman rider – well, I'm an outsider,
　But if he's a gent who the mischief's a jock?
You swells mostly blunder, Dick rides for the plunder,
　He rides, too, like thunder – he sits like a rock.

'He calls "hunted fairly" a horse that has barely
　Been stripp'd for a trot within sight of the hounds,
A horse that at Warwick beat Birdlime and Yorick,
　And gave Abdelkader at Aintree nine pounds.

'They say we have no test to warrant a protest;
　Dick rides for a lord and stands in with a steward;
The light of their faces they show him – his case is
　Prejudged and his verdict already secured.

'But none can outlast her, and few travel faster,
　She strides in her work clean away from The Drag,
You hold her and sit her she couldn't be fitter,
　Whenever you hit her she'll spring like a stag.

'And p'rhaps the green jacket, at odds though they back
　　it,
　May fall, or there's no knowing what may turn up.
The mare is quite ready, sit still and ride steady,
　Keep cool; and I think you may just win the Cup.'

Dark-brown with tan muzzle, just stripp'd for the tussle,
  Stood Iseult, arching her neck to the curb,
A lean head and fiery, strong quarters and wiry,
  A loin rather light but a shoulder superb.

Some parting injunction, bestow'd with great unction,
  I tried to recall, but forgot like a dunce,
When Reginald Murray, full tilt on White Surrey,
  Came down in a hurry to start us at once.

'Keep back in the yellow! Come up on Othello!
  Hold hard on the chestnut! Turn round on The Drag!
Keep back there on Spartan! Back you, sir, in tartan!
  So, steady there, easy,' and down went the flag.

We started, and Kerr made strong running on Mermaid,
  Through furrows that led to the first stake-and-bound,
The crack half extended look'd bloodlike and splendid,
  Held wide on the right where the headland was sound.

I pulled hard to baffle her rush with the snaffle,
  Before her two-thirds of the field got away,
All through the wet pasture where floods of the last year
  Still loitered, they clotted my crimson with clay.

The fourth fence, a wattle, floor'd Monk and Blue-bottle;
  The Drag came to grief at the blackthorn and ditch,
The rails toppled over Redoubt and Red Rover,
  The lane stopped Lycurgus and Leicestershire Witch.

She passed like an arrow Kildare and Cock Sparrow,
  And Mantrap and Mermaid refused the stone wall;
And Giles on The Greyling came down on the paling,
  And I was left sailing in front of them all.

I took them a burster, nor eased her nor nursed her
  Until the Black Bullfinch led into the plough,
And through the strong bramble we bored with a scramble –
  My cap was knock'd off by the hazel-tree bough.

Where furrows looked lighter I drew the rein tighter –
   Her dark chest all dappled with flakes of white foam,
Her flanks mud bespattered, a weak rail she shattered –
   We landed on turf with our heads turn'd for home.

Then crash'd a low binder, and then close behind her
   The sward to the strokes of the favourite shook,
His rush roused her mettle, yet ever so little
   She shorten'd her stride as we raced at the brook.

She rose when I hit her. I saw the stream glitter,
   A wide scarlet nostril flashed close to my knee,
Between sky and water The Clown came and caught her,
   The space that he cleared was a caution to see.

And forcing the running, discarding all cunning,
   A length to the front went the rider in green;
A long strip of stubble, and then the big double,
   Two stiff flights of rails with a quickset between.

She raced at the rasper, I felt my knees grasp her,
   I found my hands give to her strain on the bit,
She rose when The Clown did – our silks as we bounded
   Brush'd lightly, our stirrups clash'd loud as we lit.

A rise steeply sloping, a fence with stone coping –
   The last, we diverged round the base of the hill;
His path was the nearer, his leap was the clearer,
   I flogg'd up the straight and he led sitting still.

She came to his quarter and on still I brought her,
   And, up to his girth, to his breast-plate she drew,
A short prayer from Neville just reach'd me, 'The Devil,'
   He mutter'd – lock'd level the hurdles we flew.

A hum of hoarse cheering, a dense crowd careering,
   All sights seen obscurely, all shouts vaguely heard;
'The green wins!' 'The crimson!' The multitude swims on,
   And figures are blended and features are blurr'd.

'The horse is her master!' 'The green forges past her!'
    'The Clown will outlast her!' 'The Clown wins!' 'The
        Clown!'
The white railing races with all the white faces,
    The chestnut outpaces, outstretches the brown.

On still past the gateway she strains in the straightway,
    Still struggles 'The Clown by a short neck at most',
He swerves, the green scourges, the stand rocks and
        surges,
    And flashes, and verges, and flits the white post.

Aye! so ends the tussle – I knew the tan muzzle
    Was first, though the ring-men were yelling 'Dead
        heat!'
A nose I could swear by, but Clarke said 'The mare by
    A short head.' And that's how the favourite was beat.

≈

[167]

WILLIAM SHAKESPEARE

FROM

Henry IV part I
Act IV scene i

≈

. . . Come, let me taste my horse,
Who is to bear me like a thunderbolt.

≈

ROBERT BROWNING

How They Brought the Good News from Ghent to Aix

~

I sprang to the stirrup, and Joris, and he;
I galloped, Dirck galloped, we galloped all three;
'Good speed!' cried the watch, as the gate-bolts undrew;
'Speed!' echoed the wall to us galloping through;
Behind shut the postern, the lights sank to rest,
And into the midnight we galloped abreast.

Not a word to each other: we kept the great pace
Neck by neck, stride by stride, never changing our place;
I turned in my saddle and made its girths tight,
Then shortened each stirrup, and set the pique right,
Rebuckled the cheek-strap, chained slacker the bit,
Nor galloped less steadily Roland a whit.

'Twas moonset at starting; but while we drew near
Lokeren, the cocks crew and twilight dawned clear;
At Boom, a great yellow star came out to see;
At Düffeld, 'twas morning as plain as could be;
And from Mecheln church-steeple we heard the half-
        chime,
So Joris broke silence with, 'Yet there is time!'

At Aerschot, up leaped of a sudden the sun,
And against him the cattle stood black every one,
To stare thro' the mist at us galloping past,
And I saw my stout galloper Roland at last,
With resolute shoulders, each butting away
The haze, as some bluff river headland its spray:

And his low head and crest, just one sharp ear bent back
For my voice, and the other pricked out on his track;
And one eye's black intelligence, – ever that glance
O'er its white edge at me, his own master, askance!
And the thick heavy spume-flakes which ay and anon
His fierce lips shook upwards in galloping on.

By Hasselt, Dirck groaned; and cried Joris, 'Stay spur!
Your Roos galloped bravely, the fault's not in her,
We'll remember at Aix' – for one heard the quick wheeze
Of her chest, saw the stretched neck and staggering knees,
And sunk tail, and horrible heave of the flank,
As down on her haunches she shuddered and sank.

So we were left galloping, Joris and I,
Past Looz and past Tongres, no cloud in the sky;
The broad sun above laughed a pitiless laugh,
'Neath our feet broke the brittle bright stubble like chaff;
Till over by Dalhem a dome-spire sprang white,
And 'Gallop,' gasped Joris, 'for Aix is in sight!'

'How they'll greet us!' – and all in a moment his roan
Rolled neck and croup over, lay dead as a stone;
And there was my Roland to bear the whole weight
Of the news which alone could save Aix from her fate,
With his nostrils like pits full of blood to the brim,
And with circles of red for his eye-sockets' rim.

Then I cast loose my buffcoat, each holster let fall,
Shook off both my jack-boots, let go belt and all,
Stood up in the stirrup, leaned, patted his ear,
Called my Roland his pet-name, my horse without peer;
Clapped my hands, laughed and sang, any noise, bad or good,
Till at length into Aix Roland galloped and stood.

And all I remember is, friends flocking round
As I sat with his head 'twixt my knees on the ground;
And no voice but was praising this Roland of mine,
As I poured down his throat our last measure of wine,
Which (the burgesses voted by common consent)
Was no more than his due who brought good news from
        Ghent.

~

[169]

SIR WALTER SCOTT

FROM

Marmion
Lochinvar: Lady Heron's Song

~

O, young Lochinvar is come out of the west,
Through all the wide Border his steed was the best;
And save his good broadsword he weapons had none,
He rode all unarm'd, and he rode all alone.
So faithful in love, and so dauntless in war,
There never was knight like the young Lochinvar.

. . .

One touch to her hand, and one word in her ear,
When they reach'd the hall-door and the charger stood near;
So light to the croup the fair lady he swung,
So light to the saddle before her he sprung!
'She is won! we are gone, over bank, bush, and scaur;
They'll have fleet steeds that follow,' quoth young
        Lochinvar.

~

GEORGE WALTER THORNBURY
The Cavalier's Escape
~

Trample! trample! went the roan,
  Trap! trap! went the grey;
But pad! pad! pad! like a thing that was mad,
  My chestnut broke away.
It was just five miles from Salisbury town,
  And but one hour to day.

Thud! thud! came on the heavy roan,
  Rap! rap! the mettled grey;
But my chestnut mare was of blood so rare,
  That she showed them all the way.
Spur on! spur on! I doffed my hat,
  And wished them all good-day.

They splashed through miry rut and pool,
  Splintered through fence and rail;
But chestnut Kate switched over the gate,
  I saw them droop and tail.
To Salisbury town, but à mile of down,
  Over this brook and rail.

Trap! trap! I heard their echoing hoofs
  Past the walls of mossy stone;
The roan flew on at a staggering pace,
  But blood is better than bone.
I patted old Kate and gave her the spur,
  For I knew it was all my own.

But trample! trample! came their steeds,
  And I saw their wolf's eyes burn;
I felt like a royal hart at bay,
  And made me ready to turn.

I looked where highest grew the may,
  And deepest arched the fern.

I flew at the first knave's sallow throat;
  One blow, and he was down.
The second rogue fired twice, and missed;
  I sliced the villain's crown,
Clove through the rest, and flogged brave Kate,
  Fast, fast, to Salisbury town.

Pad! pad! they came on the level sward,
  Thud! thud! upon the sand;
With a gleam of swords, and a burning match,
  And a shaking of flag and hand.
But one long bound, and I passed the gate,
  Safe from the canting band.

~

[171]

RUDYARD KIPLING
The Ballad of East and West
~

*Oh, East is East, and West is West, and never the twain shall
    meet,*
Till Earth and Sky stand presently at God's great Judgment Seat;
But there is neither East nor West, Border, nor Breed, nor Birth,
*When two strong men stand face to face, tho' they come from the
    ends of the earth!*

Kamal is out with twenty men to raise the Borderside,
And he has lifted the Colonel's mare that is the Colonel's
    pride:

He has lifted her out of the stable-door between the dawn
        and the day,
And turned the calkins upon her feet, and ridden her far
        away.
Then up and spoke the Colonel's son that led a troop of
        the Guides:
'Is there never a man of all my men can say where Kamal
        hides?'
Then up and spoke Mahommed Khan, the son of the
        Ressaldar:
'If ye know the track of the morning-mist, ye know where
        his pickets are.
At dusk he harries the Abazai – at dawn he is into Bonair,
But he must go by Fort Bukloh to his own place to fare,
So if ye gallop to Fort Bukloh as fast as a bird can fly,
By the favour of God ye may cut him off ere he win to the
        Tongue of Jagai.
But if he be past the Tongue of Jagai, right swiftly turn ye then,
For the length and the breadth of that grisly plain is sown
        with Kamal's men.
There is rock to the left, and rock to the right, and low
        lean thorn between,
And ye may hear a breech-bolt snick where never a man
        is seen.'
The Colonel's son has taken a horse, and a raw rough dun
        was he,
With the mouth of a bell and the heart of Hell and the
        head of the gallows-tree.
The Colonel's son to the Fort has won, they bid him stay
        to eat –
Who rides at the tail of a Border thief, he sits not long at
        his meat.
He's up and away from Fort Bukloh as fast as he can fly,
Till he was aware of his father's mare in the gut of the
        Tongue of Jagai,
Till he was aware of his father's mare with Kamal upon
        her back,
And when he could spy the white of her eye, he made the
        pistol crack.

He has fired once, he has fired twice, but the whistling
      ball went wide.
'Ye shoot like a soldier,' Kamal said. 'Show now if ye can
      ride.'
It's up and over the Tongue of Jagai, as blown dust-devils
      go,
The dun he fled like a stag of ten, but the mare like a
      barren doe.
The dun he leaned against the bit and slugged his head
      above,
But the red mare played with the snaffle-bars, as a
      maiden plays with a glove.
There was rock to the left and rock to the right, and low
      lean thorn between,
And thrice he heard a breech-bolt snick tho' never a man
      was seen.
They have ridden the low moon out of the sky, their hoofs
      drum up the dawn,
The dun he went like a wounded bull, but the mare like a
      new-roused fawn.
The dun he fell at a water-course – in a woeful heap fell
      he,
And Kamal has turned the red mare back, and pulled the
      rider free.
He has knocked the pistol out of his hand – small room
      was there to strive,
' 'Twas only by favour of mine,' quoth he, 'ye rode so long
      alive:
There was not a rock for twenty mile, there was not a
      clump of tree,
But covered a man of my own men with his rifle cocked
      on his knee.
If I had raised my bridle-hand, as I have held it low,
The little jackals that flee so fast were feasting all in a
      row:
If I had bowed my head on my breast, as I have held it
      high,
The kite that whistles above us now were gorged till she
      could not fly.'

Lightly answered the Colonel's son: 'Do good to bird and
            beast,
But count who come for the broken meats before thou
            makest a feast.
If there should follow a thousand swords to carry my
            bones away,
Belike the price of a jackal's meal were more than a thief
            could pay.
They will feed their horse on the standing crop, their men
            on the garnered grain,
The thatch of the byres will serve their fires when all the
            cattle are slain.
But if thou thinkest the price be fair, – thy brethren wait
            to sup,
The hound is kin to the jackal-spawn, – howl, dog, and
            call them up!
And if thou thinkest the price be high, in steer and gear
            and stack,
Give me my father's mare again, and I'll fight my own way
            back!'
Kamal has gripped him by the hand and set him upon his
            feet.
'No talk shall be of dogs,' said he, 'when wolf and grey wolf
            meet.
May I eat dirt if thou hast hurt of me in deed or breath;
What dam of lances brought thee forth to jest at the dawn
            with Death?'
Lightly answered the Colonel's son: 'I hold by the blood
            of my clan:
Take up the mare for my father's gift – by God, she has
            carried a man!'
The red mare ran to the Colonel's son, and nuzzled against
            his breast;
'We be two strong men,' said Kamal then, 'but she loveth the
            younger best.
So she shall go with a lifter's dower, my turquoise-studded rein,
My broidered saddle and saddle-cloth, and silver stirrups
            twain.'
The Colonel's son a pistol drew and held it muzzle-end,

'Ye have taken the one from a foe,' said he; 'will ye take the
            mate from a friend?'
'A gift for a gift,' said Kamal straight; 'a limb for the risk of a
            limb.
Thy father has sent his son to me, I'll send my son to him!'
With that he whistled his only son, that dropped from a
            mountain-crest –
He trod the ling like a buck in spring, and he looked like a
            lance in rest.
'Now here is thy master,' Kamal said, 'who leads a troop of th
            Guides,
And thou must ride at his left side as shield on shoulder rides.
Till Death or I cut loose the tie, at camp and board and bed,
Thy life is his – thy fate it is to guard him with thy head.
So, thou must eat the White Queen's meat, and all her
            foes are thine,
And thou must harry thy father's hold for the peace of the
            Border-line,
And thou must make a trooper tough and hack thy way to pov
Belike they will raise thee to Ressaldar when I am hanged
            in Peshawur.'

They have looked each other between the eyes, and there
            they found no fault,
They have taken the Oath of the Brother-in-Blood on
            leavened bread and salt:
They have taken the Oath of the Brother-in-Blood on fire and
            fresh-cut sod,
On the hilt and the haft of the Khyber knife, and the
            Wondrous Names of God.
The Colonel's son he rides the mare and Kamal's boy the dun
And two have come back to Fort Bukloh where there went
            forth but one.
And when they drew to the Quarter-Guard, full twenty
            swords flew clear –
There was not a man but carried his feud with the blood
            of the mountaineer.
'Ha' done! ha' done!' said the Colonel's son. 'Put up the
            steel at your sides!

Last night ye had struck at a Border thief – tonight 'tis a
     man of the Guides!'

Oh, East is East, and West is West, and never the twain shall meet,
Till Earth and Sky stand presently at God's great Judgment Seat;
But there is neither East nor West, Border, nor Breed, nor Birth,
When two strong men stand face to face, tho' they come from the
     ends of the earth!

~

[172]

HARRY MORANT

By Warlock Hill

~

Now this is the legend of Warlock Hill,
   and thus is the story told,
Of the reckless ride of a reckless man
   who lived in the days of old,
Of the run of the fleetest brumby mare –
   and feats of a horseman bold.

When treetops shiver in wintry wind,
   and bleach 'neath the summer's sun,
A brumby mob, in the bygone years,
   in the brigalows used to run,
But they all were captured by 'Brumby Bill' –
   the whole of the mob, save one.

And this was an iron-limbed, satin-skinned brown –
   the pick of the mob, indeed!
Whene'er they had the warrigals run,
   this mare was ay in the lead;
From her tiring mates she would flash away
   through the scrub with a bullet's speed.

And in time, and in turn, had bushmen come
    from the stations far and wide,
And builded trap-yards near the waterholes,
    and many devices tried;
But the bushmen's craft and their horses' speed
    the brumby mare defied.

Yet William swore he would run that mare,
    and get her whate'er betide.
(And he and his horse were the likeliest pair
    you would find on the Border side!)
He'd sell his soul should but Satan send him
    a good enough nag to ride.

In the early dawn when fronds of pine
    were beaded with drops of dew,
Bill struck her tracks – and he followed them
    with all the craft he knew,
Till they brought him to the edge of a plain –
    with the brumby mare in view.

He raced to her side ere she crossed the plain;
    then into the scrub they dashed,
When the brigalow snapped on his saddle-pads,
    and the rotten deadwood crashed
'Neath his horse's hoofs, and the young boughs bent,
    and the brittle branches smashed.

The foam-flakes flew, and the flowers beneath
    were stained by many a fleck,
But Bill ne'er steadied, and horse ne'er fell! –
    'til little that riders reck,
When racing hard on a warrigal's flank,
    for the risk of a broken neck.

O'er plain, through scrub, by ridge and flat,
    Bill stayed beside her still;
Never a swerve from the line she took,
    and never a smash nor spill,

Till they reached to the Pelican Creek where it winds
   round the base of Warlock Hill.

Where Bill and his horse, and the brumby mare
   came down with a crashing fall
Over the bank of the Pelican Creek – 'tis of
   basalt steep and tall –
Grim, hard and grey, and some fifty feet
   is the height of that basalt wall.

Men followed their tracks next day; and they found
   the brumby dead in the sand,
With Bill and a horse (and here was a thing
   which they could not understand!)
This horse was black, and had on his hide
   what appeared like a pitchfork brand!

'He'd sell his soul for a good enough nag,'
   Bill had sworn at break o' day,
'One that could hang to the brumby mare,'
   And when he had started away,
The horse he was riding was Robin Hood –
   his favourite blood-red bay.

So there they buried that horseman bold,
   whilst the stars shone bright and chill,
And the great wan moon rose up from the cloud
   that hung over Warlock Hill;
And they carved on a gidya tree 'HERE LIES
THE BODY OF BRUMBY BILL'.

A shanty now stands upon Warlock Hill,
   and there have been travellers met,
Who, riding alone 'neath a misty moon
   when the nights were wild and wet,
Have heard the snort of the brumby mare
   and the black horse – following yet.

~

CHARLES KINGSLEY
The Knight's Leap
A Legend of Altenahr

~

'So the foemen have fired the gate, men of mine;
   And the water is spent and gone?
Then bring me a cup of the red Ahr-wine:
   I never shall drink but this one.

'And reach me my harness, and saddle my horse,
   And lead him me round to the door:
He must take such a leap tonight perforce,
   As horse never took before.

'I have fought my fight, I have lived my life,
   I have drunk my share of wine;
From Trier to Coln there was never a knight
   Led a merrier life than mine.

'I have lived by the saddle for years two score;
   And if I must die on tree,
Then the old saddle-tree, which has borne me of yore,
   Is the properest timber for me.

'So now to show bishop, and burgher, and priest,
   How the Altenahr hawk can die:
If they smoke the old falcon out of his nest,
   He must take to his wings and fly.'

He harnessed himself by the clear moonshine,
   And he mounted his horse at the door;
And he drained such a cup of the red Ahr-wine,
   As man never drained before.

He spurred the old horse, and he held him tight,
   And he leapt him out over the wall;
Out over the cliff, out into the night,
   Three hundred feet of fall.

They found him next morning below in the glen,
   With never a bone in him whole –
A mass or a prayer, now, good gentlemen,
   For such a bold rider's soul.

[174]

HENRY WADSWORTH LONGFELLOW

FROM

The Leap of Roushan Beg

Mounted on Kyrat strong and fleet,
His chestnut steed with four white feet,
Roushan Beg, called Kurroglou,
Son of the road and bandit chief,
Seeking refuge and relief,
Up the mountain pathway flew.

Such was Kyrat's wondrous speed,
Never yet could any steed
Reach the dust-cloud in his course.
More than maiden, more than wife,
More than gold and next to life
Roushan the Robber loved his horse.

. . .

Suddenly the pathway ends,
Sheer the precipice descends,
Loud the torrent roars unseen;
Thirty feet from side to side
Yawns the chasm; on air must ride
He who crosses this ravine.

Following in close pursuit,
At the precipice's foot
Reyan the Arab of Orfah
Halted with his hundred men,
Shouting upward from the glen,
'La Illah illa Allah!'

Gently Roushan Beg caressed
Kyrat's forehead, neck, and breast;
Kissed him upon both his eyes;
Sang to him in his wild way,
As upon the topmost spray
Sings a bird before it flies.

. . .

Kyrat, then, the strong and fleet,
Drew together his four white feet,
Paused a moment on the verge,
Measured with his eye the space,
And into the air's embrace
Leaped as leaps the ocean surge.

~

ADAM LINDSAY GORDON

FROM

Ye Wearie Wayfarer
Fytte I   By Wood and Wold

~

Lightly the breath of the spring wind blows,
    Though laden with faint perfume,
'Tis the fragrance rare that the bushman knows,
    The scent of the wattle bloom.
Two-thirds of our journey at least are done,
    Old horse! let us take a spell
In the shade from the glare of the noon-day sun,
    Thus far have we travell'd well;
Your bridle I'll slip, your saddle ungirth,
    And lay them beside this log,
For you'll roll in that track of reddish earth,
    And shake like a water-dog.

. . .

Fytte VII   Cito Pede Preterit Aetas

. . .

What's up, old horse? Your ears you prick,
    And your eager eyeballs glisten;
'Tis the wild dog's note in the tea-tree thick,
    By the river, to which you listen.
With head erect, and tail flung out,
    For a gallop you seem to beg,
But I feel the qualm of a chilling doubt
    As I glance at your fav'rite leg.

Let the dingo rest, 'tis all for the best,
   In this world there's room enough
For him and you and me and the rest.
   And the country is awful rough.
We've had our gallop in days of yore,
   Now down the hill we must run;
Yet at times we long for one gallop more,
   Although it were only one.

Did our spirits quail at a new four-rail,
   Could a 'double' double-bank us,
Ere nerve and sinew began to fail
   In the consulship of Plancus?
When our blood ran rapidly, and when
   Our bones were pliant and limber,
Could we stand a merry cross-counter then,
   A slogging fall over timber?

Arcades ambo! Duffers both
   In our best of days, alas!
(I tell the truth, though to tell it loth)
   'Tis time we were gone to grass;
The young leaves shoot, the sere leaves fall,
   And the old gives way to the new,
While the preacher cries, ' 'Tis vanity all,
   And vexation of spirit, too.'

. . .

Thus the measur'd stroke, on elastic sward,
   Of the steed three parts extended,
Hard held, the breath of his nostrils broad,
   With the golden ether blended;
Then the leap, the rise from the springy turf,
   The rush through the buoyant air,
And the light shock landing – the veriest serf
   Is an emperor then and there.

~

DALESMAN
Dodger's Leap
~

There, where the brook runs swift and wide,
And the banks stand grim and steep,
I once saw a flying horseman ride
And clear the lot from side to side –
A most tremendous leap!

That hedge was thick in that far-off day,
And it must have been six foot tall
When Dodger came up on his spavined grey,
Whilst we were seeking an easier way,
He gallantly cleared it all.

Now the truth of the thing we never will know,
Though we argue and talk all day,
Did poor old Dodger mean to go,
Or was old Dodger fearlessly tight,
And the old horse running away?

Had the old horse taken a sudden fright,
For he had not jumped for years;
Or was old Dodger shouting 'Whoa!'
Was he filled to the brim with the hunt's delight,
Or merely filled with beers?

The grey horse has gone where the shadows pale
And old Dodger can scarcely creep,
But still he can astound you with the tale:
How he pounded the field in the heart of the vale
At the place called 'Dodger's Leap'.

~

G. J. WHYTE-MELVILLE

FROM

The Good Grey Mare

~

They have pleached it strong, they have dug it wide,
   They have turned the baulk with the plough;
A horse that can cover the whole in its stride
   Is cheap at a thousand, I vow;
So I draw her together, and over we sail,
   With a yard and a half to spare –
Bank, bullfinch and rail – 'tis the curse of the Vale,
   But I leave it all to the mare!

. . .

I have lived my life – I am nearly done, –
   I have played the game all round;
But I freely admit that the best of my fun
   I owe it to horse and hound.
With a hopeful heart and a conscience clear,
   I can laugh in your face, Black Care;
Though you're hovering near there's no room for you
      here,
   On the back of my good grey mare.

~

WILFRID SCAWEN BLUNT
St Valentine's Day

~

Today, all day, I rode upon the Down,
With hounds and horsemen, a brave company.
On this side in its glory lay the sea,
On that the Sussex Weald, a sea of brown.
The wind was light, and brightly the sun shone,
And still we galloped on from gorse to gorse.
And once, when checked, a thrush sang, and my horse
Pricked his quick ears as to a sound unknown.
I knew the Spring was come. I knew it even
Better than all by this, that through my chase
In bush and stone and hill and sea and heaven
I seemed to see and follow still your face.
Your face my quarry was. For it I rode,
My horse a thing of wings, myself a god.

~

FELIX LEAKEY
At the Cinema

~

My mother, keen rider though she was,
Loathed and abominated hunting; for her,
Robbery with violence was bad enough,
Infanticide worse still, but hunting!
Utterly beyond the pale . . .

We were sitting together, she and I, in a Tangier cinema,
Watching a French newsreel.
Suddenly, a stag-hunt flashed on to the screen.
The grizzled old Master smiled at the camera
As horses and hounds bustled this way and that.
My mother leapt up from her seat, emitted
A stentorian 'Boo!'
                    Half-sleeping Spaniards,
Slumped back in their seats, and morosely
Puffing away at their limp *cigarillos*,
Turned their heads in amazement to gaze
At this mad Englishwoman voicing her strange protest
At some vague happening hundreds of miles away,
Which they, in Tangier, neither understood nor cared about.

But I was in torment. You see,
I understood well enough, and I knew
She was utterly *wrong*; I wanted to shout
Not 'Boo!', but 'Bravo!' What was more,
She had let us both shamefully down
In front of those sprawling foreigners. And yet, and yet
She *was* my mother, and so, to a nine-year old,
Could only be in the right.
                        I said nothing.
But still I remember, from all those long years,
How I felt, how it was.

~

ADAM LINDSAY GORDON
FROM
Ye Wearie Wayfarer
Fytte VII

≈

Yet if once we efface the joys of the chase
From the land, and outroot the Stud,
GOOD-BYE TO THE ANGLO-SAXON RACE!
FAREWELL TO THE NORMAN BLOOD!

≈

[181]

GEOFFREY CHAUCER
FROM
*The Prologue to
the Canterbury Tales*

≈

A Monk ther was, a fair for the maistrye,
An out-rydere, that lovede venerye;
A manly man, to ben an abbot able.
Ful many a deyntee hors had he in stable;
And whan he roode, men might his brydel here
Ginglen in a whistling wind as clere,
And eek as loude as dooth the chapel-belle.
Ther as this lord was keper of the celle,
. . .
He yaf not of that text a pulled hen,
That saith, that hunters been nat holy men.

≈

ROBIN IVY

The Croome Hunt at Strensham

~

Here where saint and bishop lie in silence
With knights entombed, hands stiff with prayer,
Their swords undrawn,
Time with spindly arms marks out
The clock at Strensham Court,
Leaving stump of an ancient cross
And moat of a vanished castle.

And here the hunt comes riding the green sward
Of a vanished past
To meet the crucifixion of the present.

Bit, and whip, and spur, instruments of power,
Are disciplines imposed upon the hunter;
Correct line and scent upon the hunted.

Then Gone Away they stream, the long-eared hounds
Who swarmed by polished boot, brandy brown and white,
With questioning faces.

Nose to earth, the pack in line, they strain and cry
To fill their bodies with the dwindling fox.

All at once they vanish from the hill.
Of victor and victim no sign remains,
No hammer of hooves or baying of the pack,
No tremor of twig or leaf.

Only silence. Gone Away
Where knight and saint and bishop pray
In cold grey stone.

Gone Away.

~

WILL H. OGILVIE
Between the Woods
~

Silence wraps the leafless trees,
    Not a brushwood branch is stirred;
Sleeping lies the morning breeze,
    Hidden is the listless bird.
Then – a patter in the lane;
    Then – a shoe that clicks on stone;
Creak of saddle; chink of chain;
    Music of a bit-bar thrown.

Through the lattice boughs the sun
    Sets a glittering shaft astir,
Lights the lean hounds one by one,
    Takes the bit and gilds the spur.
Right, there gleams a magpie wing;
    Left, there shrieks a watchful jay –
These have heard the deep rides ring
    Many a woodland day.

~

THOMAS MACDONAGH
FROM
The Night Hunt
~

In the morning when the sun
Burnished all the green to gorse,

I went out to take a run
Round the bog upon my horse;
And my dog that had been sleeping
In the heat beside the door
Left his yawning and went leaping
On a hundred yards before.

Through the village street we passed –
Not a dog there raised a snout –
Through the street and out at last
On the white bog road and out
Over Barna Park full pace,
Over to the Silver Stream,
Horse and dog in happy race,
Rider between thought and dream.

~

[185]

WILFRID SCAWEN BLUNT

FROM

The Old Squire

~

I like these things, and I like to ride
    When all the world is in bed,
To the top of the hill where the sky grows wide,
    And where the sun grows red.

The beagles at my horse heels trot
    In silence after me;
There's Ruby, Roger, Diamond, Dot,
    Old Slut, and Margery, –

A score of names well used, and dear,
    The names my childhood knew;
The horn, with which I rouse their cheer,
    Is the horn my father blew.

~

SIR ARTHUR CONAN DOYLE

A Hunting Morning
~

Put the saddle on the mare,
For the wet winds blow;
There's winter in the air,
    And autumn all below.
For the red leaves are flying
And the red bracken dying,
And the red fox lying
    Where the oziers grow.

Then lead round the mare,
    For it's time that we began,
And away with thought and care,
    Save to live and be a man,
While the keen air is blowing,
And the huntsman holloing,
And the black mare going
    As the black mare can.

~

EDRIC ROBERTS
The Huntsman's Horse

~

The huntsman's horse, whether brown or bay,
Or brightest chestnut, or sober grey,
Whate'er his colour, a hunting day
Is all the same to him, come what may.

When other horses, too full of beans,
Unship their riders by artful means,
Or kick each other to smithereens,
He takes no part in such ugly scenes.

He never bucks, or attempts to shy,
Or play the fool if a car goes by,
Or roll, or bolt, as do lesser fry,
On Monday mornings, when tempers fly.

He knows his job, and he's well content
To leave the frills to the 'sporting gent'
Whose hunter-chaser was never meant
For long slow hunts on a failing scent.

~

JOHN ORR EWING

FROM

A Half Section

~

How did he do it? I doubt if he knew it!
Hounds crossed the canal between Harby and Hose,
Without hesitation he took to natation,
The grey and he swam it as though they were 'pros'.

The main earths at Eaton had hounds but just beaten,
A gallant fox got there with inches to spare;
Of two hundred thrusters at Willoughby mustered,
Those two alone saw it – a man and his mare.

~

[189]

FELIX LEAKEY

A Dialogue about Hunting

~

Surely hunting is cruel?

No, it's not cruel,
In the way that so many presume: the whole pack
Converging at once and as one on the live fox
To rip him to pieces, together.

If that image is false (as you claim) – what's the true one?

The leading hound pulls the fox down,
And instantly kills him; only then comes the worry
(Which alone is what most manage ever to witness),
When your full pack arrives, then to break up the carcase.

But that wretched fox has been running
For miles and for miles for its life
Over the hostile countryside –
In the end its strength failing,
As the eager, savage pack closes in!
Isn't that cruel?

In the end (if it comes), then the fox
No doubt knows, and knows fear.
But until that time, his insouciance
Amazes, as all who have hunted will know.
He lollops along, reflectively pauses
Upon the hill, even raids the stray chicken run,
Before he steals down the hedgerow again,
To resume his casual, wily flight that more often than not
Shrugs off his pursuers, allows him
To slink back into his earth
To join mate and cubs.

Into his earth! But what then?
What of the dig, and its terror?
What of the brutal men sending their terriers down
To drive the fox out, and the terrier-man
Waiting out there, with his smile and his gun?

Those hounds have hunted hard: they deserve their fox,
If they can catch him. Then there's the farmer:
He's pleased to know now there's at least one fox fewer
To ravage his hen-run. But your thoughts, I well know,
Are all with that fox, whereas mine
Are with hounds as their nostrils fill with the glorious scent,
And their answering legs pound out the unending miles,
To fulfil their own animal destiny.

Well, you'll never get me to agree on your right
To invade the astonished fields with your horses and dogs,
There to hound a wild creature to its death,
In whatever way that may come.

So be it; let us go, then, our separate ways.
But for some – men, women, their children –
Let the countryside ring aloud still
With the horn and the tumult of hounds,
For all those whose heart leaps, whose heart quickens
To that wild, true, haunting call!

≈

[190]

VOLTAIRE

Epigram to the English

TRANSLATED BY
Olwen Way

≈

Vous fiers Anglais,
Barbare que vous êtes,
Coupez la tête aux rois
Et la queue à vos bêtes.
Mais les Français,
Polis et droits,
Aiment les lois
Laissez la queue aux bêtes
Et la tête à leurs rois.

Proud English in all things!
Barbarians that you are!

Cut off the heads of kings,
With beasts the tails you mar.
The faithful Frenchman brings
Politeness to all things.
Cutting off tails we bar,
And heads remain on kings.

~

DASHWOOD

FROM

The First Day of the Season
~

'Tis come – 'tis come – my gallant steed,
   No longer shalt thou pine;
From stall and bower today we're freed
And swift as mountain breeze shall speed
Once more, o'er hill – and mount – and mead
   Those stalwart limbs of thine!

. . .

'Tis come – 'Tis come – that soul-felt thrill!
   My straining courser bounds;
And echoing wide o'er copse and rill,
   The maddening chorus sounds!
By Heaven! He scales the distant hill!
And hark! the horn's wild summons shrill –
On! – On! – my steed! We're laggards still –
   On! – On! – my gallant hounds!

~

EDRIC ROBERTS

Seabird

He's not very young and he's not very sound,
   He's not very fast, now, they say,
But nobody knows every inch of the ground
   Like Seabird, the dealer's old grey.

He's hunted more years than I care to recall,
   He's carried us all in his day,
But no one has ever experienced a fall
   On Seabird, the dealer's old grey.

He knows the whole thing from beginning to end,
   He's artful and likes his own way,
But no one would hesitate mounting a friend
   On Seabird, the dealer's old grey.

His good reputation has spread far and wide,
    His name is a byword, today,
And every one takes quite a personal pride
    In Seabird, the dealer's old grey.

He's never been known to be sorry or sick,
    He's out from September to May;
So, here's wishing good-luck – to the very last kick –
    To Seabird, the dealer's old grey.

~

[193]

WILL H. OGILVIE
Lanyard

~

Lanyard came up looking round as a keg,
    Softer than butter and milder than milk,
Big in the body and rough in the leg;
    Now to the touch he's like satin and silk.
See him step jauntily out of his box,
    Light on his feet, with his head in the air,
Ready to race when you find him a fox –
                Limber and spare!

First he fed listlessly, missing the green,
    Slobbering over the oats that we gave,
Dreaming of meadows no more to be seen,
    Dragon-flies floating and willows that wave;
Every slow canter would drench him in sweat,
    Foam on his shoulder lay white where it starred;
Now he can gallop his miles without fret,
                Plunge and pull hard.

Long he went lazily, sluggish from grass,
    Cutting the daisies and digging his toes,
Taking no notice of aught that would pass,
    Looking no further than over his nose;
Now a far hoof-beat can set him a-dance,
    Now, by the way he takes hold of his bit,
Lanyard has waked from his long summer trance,
            – Lanyard is fit!

≈

[194]

WILLIAM BROMLEY DAVENPORT

FROM

Dream of an Old Meltonian

≈

Oh now let me know the full worth of your breeding.
Brave son of Belzoni, be true to your sires,
Sustain old traditions – remember you're leading
The cream of the cream in the Shire of the Shires!

≈

EDRIC ROBERTS

The Liver-Coloured Chestnut

~

He never seemed to have a name,
Like others in the Stable job,
But from the day when first he came
Was called the liver-chestnut cob,
And always, since, remained the same.

He soon acquired a modest fame
For confidence and commonsense;
Was never sorry, sick or lame,
Or wantonly refused a fence,
But took them all just as they came.

His hardy coat and sturdy frame
Grew more familiar up in front,
For keeness made his constant aim
To see the finish of a hunt,
Which few, as oft as he, could claim.

And every Season he became
A greater equine personage;
And, full of honours and acclaim,
He lived until a ripe old age,
The chestnut cob without a name.

~

JOHN MASEFIELD

FROM

Reynard the Fox

~

A chestnut mare with swerves and heaves
Came plunging, scattered all the crowd,
She tossed her head and laughed aloud
And bickered sideways past the meet.
From pricking ears to mincing feet
She was all tense with blood and quiver,
You saw her clipt hide twitch and shiver
Over her netted cords of veins.
She carried Cothill, of the Sleins,
A tall, black, bright-eyed, handsome lad.
Great power and great grace he had.
Men hoped the greatest things of him.

~

FELIX LEAKEY

Hounds Running

~

A lawn meet: the avenue snaked with its horses,
Spilling out from their trailers, backed out with much
      shouting
And 'whoa's' on to tarmac thick-strewn with manure;
Hoick into the saddle, then clippety-clop!
In a frisky procession.

The drive fronting the house; an ear-splitting tumult;
Shouted greetings and badinage, mounts reconnoitred,
As helpers ply to and fro, smilingly proffering
Goblets and sandwiches, sausage rolls, weather lore:
'Bit of rain in the offing; good scent, whaddya think?'
Some dismount, casting reins to stray friends, striding over
Lawns trampled already, by boot and by hoof,
Through French windows flung open to more piled-up
          provender.

Now hounds and hunt horses stream into the driveway:
A raised whip, a doffed cap, and 'Have a care, you!',
As the strays from the pack nose around in the flower-beds.
Mounted throng sidles outwards: a ripple of scarlet,
Of sober black, ratcatcher, top hat and bowler,
Of hunt cap, stretch breeches, boots polished and
          spurred,
Gloved hands folded round a neat-trailing whip,
And at each throat a froth of white puffed out and brilliant.
O the heart-easing grace of the side-saddle ladies,
And their cross-saddle counterparts: elegant, trim!

Here's the foot brigade, threading its way through the
          horses:
Sheepskin, anorak, tied scarf and flat cap;
The children, by two-legged hounds inundated,
Delightedly fondling each paw on each shoulder,
Each wistful hound-muzzle that stretches and nuzzles.

A scene quintessential, as English as Shakespeare!
Of legends the stuff; dare we cast it away
Through mere canting hypocrisy?

But it's time to move off – more than time, for the Master
Has glanced at the huntsman, moved forward and uttered
His time-honoured signal: 'Hounds, gentlemen, please!'
And already they're on to the high road; we follow,
And find a new rhythm, a quick-striding cadence:
Trit-trot! Up and down! We edge our way forwards,

With smiles and with chatter. The covert at last:
We take up our positions, horses' heads to the wind,
As hounds scatter all over.

From the wood, a deep silence; from us, subdued murmurs,
A shuffling of hooves and a jingling of harness.
Puppies shrill, are cursed quiet by their huntsman; a burst
Of hound music; a crashing of tongues,
As it swells, as it deepens;
A screech from the hillside; an answering holloa;
They pour from the thicket, and we thunder after!

Abreast on the hillside, then fanning out widely,
Each one for himself, yet each one united
In unspoken fellowship driving us on
Over grass, over fence, skirting ploughed field and covert.
But all at once: check! Riders now a mere handful –
More by luck than good judgment, myself still among them.
Down there, by the quarry, hounds puzzle it out,
Casting this way and that, while the huntsman stays silent:
He's right, for they're on again, voices rebounding
From cliff wall as upwards they toil to fresh country,
And after them galloping, galloping, galloping,
We fly over the grassland! But the edge of a wood
Brings our mounts to a standstill;
We lose hounds and impetus, jumping in, jumping out,
Taking breath, swigging brandy, collapsed in our saddles,
And away in the distance hear hounds speaking still.

A mile or two on, so we hear, they have killed –
As twice more on that golden, that high-scented day.
With respect we salute from afar each quick death,
With its rites immemorial, its age-old despatch.

At the end of the day, we turn horses for home.
Tired limbs slump in the saddle, reins droop from our fingers,
As we thoughtfully plod through the softly damp darkness
To the stables, the warmth and the welcoming bath.

≈

ALFRED MUNNINGS

FROM

The Cottesmore Ball

~

And standing there at her horse's side
Was the girl who had shown us the way to ride;
The fair Lizette, who had led the hunt
On her gallant horse, a field in front;
A field in front without a fault;
But any horse that was worth its salt
Was twice the horse if he should get
The chance to carry the fair Lizette.

Lizette was up on her horse again;
I watched them moving along the lane,
Jogging upon the grass-grown verge;
The horse, now feeling the homeward urge
Stirring within his horse's soul,
Chaffing against her mild control,
Gave to Lizette that poise so rare,
That was hers alone beyond compare.
The cut of her habit showed the line
Of the perfect female form divine,
And every line displayed her grace. . . .
. . .
Throughout the run the foremost place
Being hers, there scarce was sign of dirt
Or splash of clay on her habit skirt;
No mark or speck on the black silk hat,
Her hair still smooth in a glossy plait. . . .
. . .
Here was the girl who had made the pace –
A true Diana of the Chase! . . .

~

[199]
WILL H. OGILVIE
Hacking Home
~

When your homing carloads swing
  Past us down the crisping lanes,
And your dazzling headlights fling
  Snow-white roses on our reins,
Would we choose your sheltered flight,
  Would we take your cushioned ease
For the wide and scented night
  And the horse between our knees?

Breezes that your wheels o'erleap
  Whisper round us as we ride;
Ours the star-bedusted deep
  That your misted windows hide;
And while speed may waft you soon
  To your halls of warmth and light,
Is not ours the magic moon
  Spilling silver from the night?

~

ALISON BRACKENBURY
Homecoming
~

Horses have quick routes they know
A few safe roads, on which they always go,
They are not tempted by the sudden lane
The silver poplar shivering in light.
They only crave heaped hay again,
And pull to keep the low white yard in sight.

So I must fight them, if I am to go
On fruitless roads, on past the dulling tree;
Nor could I tell them, even if I knew
What it was we turned so far to see,
Before the hungry stables of the night.

~

ALFRED MUNNINGS
FROM
Larkbarrow Farm, Exmoor
~

And all those folk who've had their day
Step into their cars and drive away;
    Their horses taken home by grooms,
By many a moorland track and path,
Whilst they themselves lie in the bath,

With reek of bath salts in their rooms,
And dress themselves beside the fire.
But what of the man in wet attire
   And dripping hat who begins to tire,
   On his weary way to Larkbarrow?

Ere he was well on his homeward track,
And walking to ease his horse's back,
   A fog o'erspread that sodden waste, –
A cloak of grey wrapped all around:
And as he walked, the only sound
   Was water running down in haste,
Pouring along beside the way.
He longed to see the clearing day
   And the lettered name on the gate to say
   He was home again at Larkbarrow.

And as he looked he saw no sign
Of track on the moors to give his line;
   The horse had stopped with a fearful snort:
Fearing the ground, he rode again,
And gave the plodding beast the rein,
   And soon its guiding instinct brought
The rider safe, though rather late,
Up to that welcome, whitened gate,
   With its lettered name as sure as fate,
   Which led to the farm at Larkbarrow.

~

EDRIC ROBERTS
Blessings
~

Hacking home in the moonlight, slowly,
    You and I on the silver road,
Tired and stiff, but contented wholly
    With the blessings the day bestowed.

Blessings worthy their own recording
    In the pages of Memory;
But the best and the most rewarding
    Is, old pal, how you carried me.

~

WILL H. OGILVIE
Storm-Stayed
~

When snowflakes are whirling and highways are drifted,
When hounds are in kennel and nags in their stalls;
When the centre of faith to the fireside has shifted
And life is confined within four solid walls;
Then Memory for comfort stands touching our shoulder,
And Fancy for favour sits close by our side,
And drifts may pile deeper and winds may grow colder,
But down in our hearts there are green fields to ride.

With the smoke from our pipes like a meadow mist trailing,
With the hum of the storm-wind like hoofs in our ears,

Across the big pastures in dream we go sailing
To pound the reluctant and pace with our peers;
Or, stretched on the sofa, we sup with the sages;
With Nimrod, or Surtees the second to none;
Or search through the Druid's delectable pages,
Or sample with Brooksby the Best of the Fun.

For some there are scenes of their youth to recover;
Wild musters, wild round-ups in sage brush and sand,
From the fenceless far places that lack not a lover
So long as the snaffle lies light to the hand.
Though snowflakes be whirling, and highways be drifted,
Though hounds doze in kennel and nags in their stalls,
There's never a storm-cloud too dark to be lifted
When dream-logs are burning in horse-lovers' halls.

~

[204]

ALISON BRACKENBURY
Snowbound
~

The horses skidded on the black-iced road
Stiff-legged as skiers, snorting the raw air.
The sheep and lambs lay quiet in the fields,
Bundles of grey, against the miles of snow.
Hock-deep, the horses floundered through the gate
Mistrusting the steep track they used to know.

Blue, the tall young hunter, climbed ahead
Breasting the drifts, tossing and plunging deep.
The soft snow caved around him, poured and echoed
A dull white thunder on the icy hill.
So my horse stiffened, fumbling in the craters:
The small grey pony? Can he manage? Still

Charging the slope, below the drifts, on hard
Horse-trodden snow, he scrambled up behind
His mane gold-glinting, like a dandelion,
Against such brightness, bristling at the cold,
He came, fastest of all, and his eyes shone.

Blue stumbled in a dip, sank to the chest.
'We can't go through,' his rider called. To that
The file fidgeted: Paddy, the best
At jumping, and the grey horse who will pull,
Run off for miles – whipped down sudden heads
Into blue-shadowed folds, to sink, to roll.

Their frightened riders tugged their reins up hard,
Swung round – What had they seen? No earth, no grass –
They had been stabled now for months – what glare
Or perfect promise in the glittered field?

We edged back down our path, left snow's loud falls behind,
Hooves scraped off the firm road. 'Horses are mad!' we said,
Miles out, from heat and home, out in the high, east wind.

~

[205]

OLWEN WAY
To Cymro
~

The strange, wild sunset tempted me
To ride to the woods today
(I watched your hoof-prints in the snow
And listened as you breathed).
And the ice clamped round us with bitter scorn

Resenting us, and you reared in alarm
At the scream on the wind,
And snorted at the smell.
Celt that you are, your fears I know
Of mystery and magic spell
(I watched your hoof-prints in the snow).
But the scream on the wind was the tortured trees
And the smell on the wind was the storm.
And the white white shrouds of the snow-smoothed land
Had thick dark cords, like a tough rope band
Where the plough reared starkly.
Alien unfriendly earth, blind, treacherous ditch
And torturing air, foreboding wind and haunting trees
We conquered you.
(I watched his hoof-prints in the snow.)

~

[206]

ROBERT FROST

Stopping by Woods on a Snowy Evening
~

Whose woods these are I think I know.
His house is in the village, though;
he will not see me stopping here
To watch his woods fill up with snow.

My little horse must think it queer
To stop without a farmhouse near
Between the woods and frozen lake
The darkest evening of the year.

He gives his harness bells a shake
To ask if there is some mistake.
The only other sound's the sweep
Of easy wind and downy flake.

The woods are lovely, dark, and deep,
But I have promises to keep,
And miles to go before I sleep,
And miles to go before I sleep.

~

[207]

MAURICE LINDSAY
The Fall of the Leaf

~

As I rode home through woods that smelled of evening,
my horse reined up on his intuitive will
and stood, ears cocked, hearing his visible breathing,
the only sound alive this side the hill.
Autumn hung by a silence, swollen full
of the year's roundness. Under spars of dusk
the encircling frost moved stealthily to snick
each brittle stalk and shrivel night's black husk.

As if somehow it sensed its enemy
the tired air leant against the lingering light,
trembling accumulated scents upon
the rearguard shadows backing the sun's flight.
Torn by the last horizon's hedgerow, strips
of straggled brightness littered the rutted track,
glossing a pack of ragged crows who savaged
hunger's edge with their own caw and clack.

It was as if the shorn and trampled season
bared an epiphany with no savioured parts
for we who hanker after permanence
while boredom and desires burn out our hearts:
until his tenseness splintered in a whinney,
acknowledging a cue I could not hear,
and anapaesting down his instinct's treason,
his hoofbeats thumped a rhyme of fear and dare.

≈

[208]

WILLIAM COWPER

FROM

The Task
Snow

≈

Ill fares the traveller now, and he that stalks
In ponderous boots beside his reeking team.
The wain goes heavily, impeded sore
By congregated loads adhering close
To the clogged wheels; and in its sluggish pace
Noiseless appears a moving hill of snow.
The toiling steeds expand the nostril wide,
While every breath, by respiration strong
Forced downward, is consolidated soon
Upon their jutting chests. He, formed to bear
The pelting brunt of the tempestuous night,
With half-shut eyes and puckered cheeks, and teeth
Presented bare against the storm, plods on.
One hand secures his hat, save when with both
He brandishes his pliant length of whip,
Resounding oft, and never heard in vain.

≈

WILLIAM MORRIS

FROM

The Haystack in the Floods

~

Along the dripping leafless woods,
The stirrup touching either shoe,
She rode astride as troopers do;
With kirtle kilted to her knee,
To which the mud splashed wretchedly;
And the wet dripped from every tree
Upon her head and heavy hair,
And on her eyelids broad and fair;
The tears and rain ran down her face.
By fits and starts they rode apace,
And very often was his place
Far off from her; he had to ride
Ahead, to see what might betide
When the roads crossed; and sometimes, when
There rose a murmuring from his men,
Had to turn back with promises;
Ah me! she had but little ease;
And often from pure doubt and dread
She sobbed, made giddy in the head
By the swift riding; while, for cold,
Her slender fingers scarce could hold
The wet reins; yea, and scarcely, too,
She felt the foot within her shoe
Against the stirrup . . .

~

ROBERT BROWNING

The Last Ride Together

~

Then we began to ride. My soul
Smooth'd itself out, a long-cramp'd scroll
Freshening and fluttering in the wind.
Past hopes already lay behind.
  What need to strive with a life awry?
Had I said that, had I done this,
So might I gain, so might I miss.
Might she have loved me? just as well
She might have hated, who can tell!
Where had I been now if the worst befell?
  And here we are riding, she and I.

. . .

And yet – she has not spoke so long!
What if heaven be that, fair and strong
At life's best, with our eyes upturn'd
Whither life's flower is first discern'd,
  We, fix'd so, ever should so abide?
What if we still ride on, we two
With life for ever old yet new,
Changed not in kind but in degree,
The instant made eternity, –
And heaven just prove that I and she
  Ride, ride together, for ever ride?

~

E. LADSON
Pony-Trek
~

Crisp autumn morning with a pale sun peering,
  Picking out the highlights on chestnut, black, and bay,
Ten keen trekkers and their ten wise ponies,
  Stringing out along the road to start a trekking day.

Start off soberly, steady on the tarmac,
  (Walk, mare, walk!) till we're fairly out of town.
Now the leader's trotting on (bring 'em up behind, there!)
  Rising to the rhythm with your hands well down.

Splash through a shallow stream – stop and take a drink,
          nag,
  Brush through the heather where the late bees hum;
Clamber up the sheep-track snaking round the hillside,
  Easy now, pony! there's a steeper bit to come.

Wind along the gorsy moor, sitting nice and easy,
  Slither down the stony path, slipping on the scree;
Steal a little canter where the turf lies smoothly,
  Stop and let her graze where the grass springs free.

Gently down the home hill (oats begin to call, lass?)
  Clatter through the stable-yard – feeding will be fun.
Ten tired trekkers and their ten tired ponies,
  Hungry, hot, and happy with a good day done.

~

ALFRED MUNNINGS

An Exmoor Lane

This little pony poem was written after meeting a herd in the lane
leading from Withypool village to the Moor, one of the territories
of that herd of ponies.

~

Grey leaden clouds, slow moving overhead;
The trees and fences dripping as I pass;
A robin singing; berries turning red;
And underfoot the rank and sodden grass.

And all is shrouded in soft, misty rain;
And spattering drops are falling through the beech;
Still puddles lie along the rutted lane
In long, light streaks of grey which curve and reach

Between the fences, 'neath the rainy sky;
And calm, unbroken silence spreads around,
Save for the far-off rook's and jackdaw's cry
And sound of ceaseless rain upon the ground.

But hark! I hear the sound of unshod feet!
And ponies come in sight ten yards ahead:
We stare at one another as we meet,
And suddenly there's silence like the dead!

With pricked-up ears, bright eye and flowing mane,
The older ones amongst them seem to say
'You cannot stop us coming up the lane;
For centuries we've used this right of way.'

Those hurrying feet are stayed; – We stand and stare.
Then, as I draw aside to let them go,
The leader dashes by – an ancient mare,
And all the rest with mane and tail aflow

Go charging by in vigorous life and strength;
Bright startled eyes and forelocks blowing back;
Sturdy and stout, they gallop up the length
Of the long lane towards the moorland track:

And as I watch them galloping away;
The rain and dying bracken all forgot;
I feel how weak am I, how strong are they:
Theirs is a life of freedom, mine is not.

They disappear and leave me where I stand
Alone and wondering at the passing sight,
As seen a hundred times in this wild land –
And often on a dark and eerie night

When folk are fast asleep and many snore,
You hear the hurried sound of unshod feet,
Of ponies as they change from moor to moor,
All rushing through the narrow village street.

They know no bounds, they wander where they will;
They graze beside the stream that babbles by;
When days are hot, they stand upon the hill –
A silhouetted group against the sky.

And in the spring the little foals are born,
And there they lie, all basking in the heat
Of some gorse-scented, blazing April morn,
Upon the close-cropped grass where ponies' feet

Have trodden on their way across the moor
Down to the running stream year after year.
A venerable grand-dam going on before,
The stallion always bringing up the rear.

~

THE KORAN

~

Verily, blessing is tied to the forelocks of horses
unto the judgement day.

~

TUDOR ALED

FROM

To Ask For A Stallion

TRANSLATED BY
Gwyn Williams

~

Lewis, son of Madoc, boldly
will now ask for a stallion.
He's a soldier between Maelor and Rhos,
and closely linked with Tegeingl.
He wishes to have, ready for May,
a pretty girl and a horse to carry her.
For a poem he seeks one with a stag's look,
a dimple-nosed one turning in his tunic,
a bear's nostril, a moving mouth,
a bridle holding his nose in a loop,
a nose which holds the bridle when we curb him,
the hollow nostril like the muzzle of a gun.
Eyes that are like two pears,
lively and keen, they leap from his head;
two slim and restless ears,

like sage leaves at his forehead;
like polishing of gems
was the glazier's dressing of his hooves;
brisk on four sets of eight nails,
with a spark from every nail's head.
His coat is like new silk,
his hair might be tree gossamer,
silk of a skylark's tunic
and camlet covering a young stag.
He spins without use of hands
and weaves a kerchief of silk.
Strong-waisted foal biting the highway,
the fair's alarm, out of his way!
His liveliness we liken
to a red fawn before the hounds.
He's such a lusty creature
that he floats to his purpose;
to make him prance you'll never
need to put steel to his belly;
under a brisk, keen horseman
he always knows his mind;
leaping over where the thorns are greatest,
full of attack in Llan Eurgain.
If he's ridden over to the hayfield
he won't break eight stalks with his hoof.
Stirring to the thunder's course,
and mincingly stepping where he pleases,
he'd throw a leap at the sky,
he'd fly in confidence,
and if we ride him over a wall
this prince's horse will run on.
A battering ram winding up the hill,
he throws his nailheads to the sun;
sparks fly from every hoof,
eight points are pierced into each one;
there are stars or lightning on the road
at the lifting of his fetlocks.
Like a stag with fiercest gaze,
his feet weave through wild fire;

he jumps across a river
like a roebuck jumping from a snake.
Is there better payment for such a fawn
than praise of the slim beast?
There's a maiden, a beauty waiting for me,
if I had a horse to carry her off.
The best speed ever made was by
a good horse bearing a pretty girl.

~

[215]

FELIX LEAKEY
On the Haystack
~

My mother had come home from riding; she still
Had her boots on, and over her head
Wore a floppy felt hat.

As I hurried my way through the gateway to meet her,
She jumped off her horse, left him there quite untethered,
And scooped me up in her arms, to run headlong, full tilt,
Over dry summer grass to the haystack nearby.
We fell down together, both laughing, entwined in each
          other,
And into the sweet-smelling hay we rolled over and over,
And over, and over, and over . . .
Nothing more happened, you understand. (I was only
          five.)

But for me, everything happened.

~

[216]

PHILIP SIDNEY

FROM

Sonnet 84

~

Highway, since you my chief Parnassus be,
   And that my Muse, to some ears not unsweet,
Tempers her words to trampling horses' feet
   More oft than to a chamber melody, –
Now blessèd you bear onward blessèd me
   To her, where I my heart, safe-left, shall meet.

~

[217]

ALFRED, LORD TENNYSON

FROM

The Princess

~

. . . And the last, my other heart,
And almost my half-self, for still we moved
Together, twinn'd as horse's ear and eye.
. . .
With stroke on stroke the horse and horseman came
As comes a pillar of electric cloud.

~

[218]

WILLIAM SHAKESPEARE

FROM

Macbeth
Act III scene i

~

I wish your horses swift and sure of foot;
And so I do commend you to their backs.

~

SIR MICHAEL WILLIAM SELBY BRUCE
My Choice in Life
~

Let me lead my life in the saddle,
It's the life to which I've been bred;
  It's the life of the wise
  With only the skies,
The wonderful skies, overhead.

Let me lead my life in the saddle,
With a horse and a dog as my friend;
  With a horse and a gun
  I'll get the best run
Till I come to my final end.

Let me end my life in the saddle,
On a horse all out in its stride;
  Let a sudden fall
  Be the end of all
O'er a ditch that's both deep and wide.

~

GERARD MANLEY HOPKINS

FROM

Felix Randal

~

Felix Randal, the farrier, O he is dead then? . . .

. . .

How far from then forethought of, all thy more boisterous
  years,
When thou at the random grim forge, powerful amidst
  peers,
Didst fettle for the great grey drayhorse his bright and
  battering sandal!

~

[221]

GUILLAUME DE SALLUSTE DU BARTAS

Moonwort

On the old superstition that purple honesty or 'moonwort' had the
power of drawing the shoes from horses.

~

And horse that, feeding on the grassy hills,
Tread upon moonwort with their hollow heels,
Though lately shod at night goe barefoot home,
Their maister musing where their shooes become.
O moonwort! tell us where thou hidst the smith,
Hammer, and pincers, thou unshod'st them with?

Alas! what lock or engine is't
That can thy subtile secret strength resist,
Sith the best farrier cannot set a shoe
So sure, but thou (so shortly) canst undo?

~

[222]

ANONYMOUS

Horse Lore: A Devonshire Rhyme
~

If you have a horse with four white legs,
Keep him not a day;
If you have a horse with three white legs,
Send him far away;
If you have a horse with two white legs,
Sell him to a friend;
If you have a horse with one white leg,
Keep him to the end.

~

THOMAS DE GRAY

FROM

The Compleat Horse-Man and Expert Ferrier
2nd edn 1651

Thomas de Gray quotes a 'famous farrier of Paris' and himself translated from French verse these lines on the colour of a good horse.

~

If you desire a horse thee long to serve,
Take a browne-bay, and him with care preserve:
The gray's not ill, but he is prized far
That is cole-black, and blazoned with a star:
If for thyselfe, or friend, thou wilt procure
A horse, let him white-Lyard be, He'l long endure.

~

[224]

LI PO

A Roan Horse

TRANSLATED BY
Richard King

~

The roan horse gallops along and neighs,
His green jade hoofs a blur of speed.
Nearing the river, he wishes not to cross
As though anxious for his brocade mudflaps.

The cities of the Pai-hsüeh are far away in the passes,
The Huang-yun barbarians from the sea are scattered.
At the flick of a whip he will go ten thousand li,
Why should he long for Spring to return?

~

[225]

BILL WALROND

Show Fever
With apologies to John Masefield

~

I must go out to a show again
I really don't know why.
And all I ask is a tandem cart
And some reins to steer it by.
And the Wheeler kicks
And it all goes wrong
With the sound of a shaft breaking –
And a broad grin
On the Leader's face
And the Wheeler overtaking.

~

JOHN BETJEMAN
Hunter Trials

~

It's awf'lly bad luck on Diana,
Her ponies have swallowed their bits;
She fished down their throats with a spanner
And frightened them all into fits.

So now she's attempting to borrow.
Do lend her some bits, Mummy, *do*;
I'll lend her my own for tomorrow,
But today *I*'ll be wanting them too.

Just look at Prunella on Guzzle,
The wizardest pony on earth;
Why doesn't she slacken his muzzle
And tighten the breech in his girth?

I say, Mummy, there's Mrs Geyser
And doesn't she look pretty sick?
I bet it's because Mona Lisa
Was hit on the hock with a brick.

Miss Blewitt says Monica threw it,
But Monica says it was Joan,
And Joan's very thick with Miss Blewitt,
So Monica's sulking alone.

And Margaret failed in her paces,
Her withers got tied in a noose,
So her coronets caught in the traces
And now all her fetlocks are loose.

Oh, it's me now, I'm terribly nervous.
I wonder if Smudges will shy.

She's practically certain to swerve as
Her pelham is over one eye.

*   *   *

Oh wasn't it naughty of Smudges?
Oh, Mummy, I'm sick with disgust.
She threw me in front of the Judges,
And my silly old collarbone's bust.

~

[227]

BETTY STONEHAM

An Ode to the Shetland Pony

~

You stood upon the springy turf
So small and yet so strong,
You gazed at me with gentle eyes,
And as you idly swished those flies
That flew in never ending streams –
I saw the idol of my dreams.

~

WILL H. OGILVIE
Ponies for Islington
~

Ponies, ponies for Islington! The patter of eager hoofs
Rings through the London arches and dies in the London
        roofs;
Ponies following ponies, hogmaned, clipped and dressed,
Ranelagh's pride and beauty, Hurlingham's picked and
        best.

Lords of the world's gymkhanas, heroes of bending fame;
Bred to the tireless gallop, made to the perfect game;
Mouthed to the lightest handling, ribbed to carry a weight,
Ready to wheel at a whisper, ready to turn on a plate.

Ponies fresh from the cloud-mist on the high green hills of
        Wales,
Brecon mud on their shoulders, Appynt fern in their tails,
Wild-eyed, wonderful-crested roans and bays and greys
Lone for the Irfon River and the old remembered ways.

Ponies up from the Forest, startled and swift and shy,
Fresh from the glades of Lyndhurst where the watchful
        roebuck lie;
Foaled in the blackthorn thickets that look to the Channel
        tides;
Wild as the hawks that hover over the Beaulieu rides.

Ponies down from the Shetlands, wards of the treeless plain,
Hard as the salted sea breeze, dour as the driving rain;
Tossing their tangled forelocks, nursing an ample pride
In all they have done for England in teaching her sons to ride.

Garrons bred where the birches cling to the mountain glen,
Full of the fiery courage they share with the Highland men;

Yellows and duns and creamies, marked with the line of jet –
The long black line that was never the badge of a bad one yet!

Ponies bred on the moorlands above the Exe and Dart,
Threading the crowded traffic with high undaunted heart,
Wisdom that skirts the bog-land, courage that climbs the tor,
Brought from Dunkery Beacon to lead them in London's roar.

Hark to the stallions neighing! Hark to the trampling feet!
Beauty bent to the lead-rein sidling along the street! –
Tide on the shores of Shetland lashing the sea-rocks rude,
Call of the wind on Snowdon, scent of the Horner Wood!

~

[229]

RUDYARD KIPLING

FROM

A Smuggler's Song

~

If you wake at midnight, and hear a horse's feet,
Don't go drawing back the blind, or looking in the street,
Them that asks no questions isn't told a lie.
Watch the wall, my darling, while the Gentlemen go by!
Five and twenty ponies,
Trotting through the dark –
Brandy for the Parson,
'Baccy for the Clerk;
Laces for a lady, letters for a spy,
Watch the wall, my darling, while the Gentlemen go by!

~

GWERFYL MECHAIN
The Grey Steed

TRANSLATED BY
A. P. Graves

~

Dost thou need a swift grey steed,
These points in him are owing –
Coat short and clean – belly lean –
Mane like tresses flowing;
Each unwearying, twinkling ear
Erect and neatly narrow;
Nostrils red as fire, that shed
Foam showers o'er field and furrow;
Neck arched and strong, nose fine and long,
Thin hoofs that sparkles scatter
Down the street, as ring on ring
They stamp with singing clatter!

~

ALISON BRACKENBURY
Welsh Song

~

Glen, small, bay horse: since I complained
Of your short name, we have devised a long
New title to which you may trot in time;
Glendower, quick, red horse, I will give you a Welsh song.
First we will declare that you are not
The dark racehorse whose shoulder I just touch
Who eats the hill in seven strides; or such
A brave white mare as Martha, whose great trot
Called to the morning streets through which I rode.
You are bored by walk and circling, in the covered school;
Will you lighten, if I take you to the hill,
Where, cantering this day, you sprang aside,
Tore past the others, flattening corn? and still
Shaking, on safe paths I vowed to have you.
Through the high Welsh summer, I rode a small black mare
Who loped her heather like a cat, dodged through
The dripping woods, all ease – To take you there –
Would that be Paradise? Yet she had, too
Her terror: one car, crawling the hill, sent her
Scrambling the bank, through pigeons, wet gold moss.

That was a strange company – the dentist's English wife
With her light voice and her young careful hair,
Pleading boredom, riding with a college friend
A slim man, going grey. And yelling, everywhere
Galloping – the wild girl off the farm
Whose quiet sister waded, in the leaf-dark stream,
Which gave their water, which was running low:
Brown fingers cleared the pipe, searched out the source:
So in red rains, past heat of engines, we
Will see your quick land run, Glendower my horse.

~

OLWEN WAY

On Showing a Welsh Pony

~

Beauty wove for me a woof,
Streaming mane and racing cloud –
Rain drenched turf and eager hoof
History, folklore, legend, myth,
Beauty works serene in this
Weaving where, with joy she can
Use for thread the natural law –
God, in partnership with man.

~

EDRIC ROBERTS

Kildare

~

At the Shows, in full swing,
All the Summer and Spring,
    The select and elect
Of the stars in the Ring,
Very few could compare
With the four-year-old mare
    Which they said
    Had been bred
In the County Kildare.

Later on, in the height
Of the Season, the sight,
        At the Meet, was a treat,
Of the dashing First Flight,
Yet not one could compare
With the stylish bay mare
        Which was bred,
        So they said,
In the County Kildare.

That great day, when they soon
Found a fox, after noon,
        Ran to kill, on the hill,
By the light of the moon,
The only one there
Was that smashing bay mare,
        Truly said
        To've been bred
In the County Kildare.

WILL H. OGILVIE
To You

~

Here's to you, Stocking and Star and Blaze!
You brought me all that the best could bring –
Health and Mirth and the Merriest Days
In the Open Fields and the Woodland Ways –
And what can I do in return, but sing
A song or two in your praise!

~

ALISON BRACKENBURY
Five Horses: Excerpts from Breaking Ground
Captain

~

Though he is not the oldest; though his coat's
still fine, red-gold, he dozes in his stall,
short sandy lashes shut: soft though you coax
only a shoulder twitches, to each call.
Nothing wakes him, stiff as an old general,
the last reserve, the horse which you'd first ride
whose long forelegs still strike out with some grace
but hind legs check – oh rocking horse! – each stride.

I thought him patient, watched him stoop and still,
while girls bound cloth about each swollen leg;
until we galloped on the winter hill
of harsh and stony ground; were overtaken
by every horse. Pulled up then, at the rear
he laid his red ears flat, struck from the path
still steamed, sweat-dark, pushed hard to jostle through
to the ride's head, the place he meant to be.

Watch close: is he asleep? Yellow and savage
are teeth his twitched lips bare. His lamed, slim feet
shudder in straw. Though he is gelded, as
stallions to a March cry rear and thrash,
he pounds the gathered dark, out-races age.

~

Paddy

~

Paddy, first owned, was barely fed,
his ribs jabbed through
hair dull as mud;
now his brown belly swells
broader than barrels
he grunts while trotting,
crossly, skids
wild across the school –
no warning –

no one's fool
comes hard to learning:
                        Jumps the moon
in pictures shown,
in blue and frost's air
sailing
(though thick-legged as beasts you coaxed
round hedge, dark pondside, ploughing)

from the hay-heaps his rams and cries
scatter rough ponies, reeling:

The horses – twice his weight, and size –
                        From his low nose
Run squealing.

~

Patrick

His wall eye stares, white crystal, blue:
is pure – and cold. Does Patrick think?
High as walls stand; whitening slow
(as greys do, ageing) to instincts
he has added swerves and falls
red jags of pain he would not come to
willingly, once more. So Patrick
I trust most: to come straight home:

Measuring mud, the gate's width: speed:
Jumping, always, as he's asked to:
Doing all things if he trusts you –

Never trust such dignity.
It is Patrick who I see
Die willingly: on hunting ground
           Set to high walls; white legs unsound.

Oscar

~

There are lists of horses' habits,
weaving, dishing and crib-biting
all are strange, their names exciting,
most are wretched: like wind-sucking –
to breathe in, wrongly, just because it
bores you, breathing. Oscar does it.

Simply stated, it can kill you.
Oscar once must have been bored
near to death, left in a stable.
Now his breath comes gurgling through
swallowed, stifling: who affords
such luxury outside a fable?

Real breath chokes you, held inside –
as he would not be, small horse, racing
even wild Monty down,
warm and strong horse, drumming, breasting
cold wind, thistles. And then, bored;

Straps tied round his neck to keep him
out of the familiar hurting
hold him back from solaced eating
silent, fretting,
passion, flawed.

~

Monty

I would tell you at last,
of purest madness
of horses I saw first:
the thoroughbred,
Dancer who came
from desert Arabians,
wild as time –
and hopelessly inbred.

Forget the pride in trappings,
the money, the long names
of owners: straw and cloths
stamped by their feet:
they do not belong by furs and paddocks.
From crooked, blazing light
They rise and leap.

Never would I ride one
the gods must make you mad –
happy to die young.
Monty, the black horse, fires
at sight of open country, whirls through sun
plunges at barbed wire:

was once a show-jumper, once broke a leg:
will kill a man, I think. I watch, and sense –
from Patrick's back – a golden field about him
electrical. He's lost. He is the distance

In the grass fields we meet. He's gentle there.
He has the soft nose of the Arab, slight
dropped to a hand. Only his far eye looks
Past gates and apples, to the speed of light.

[236]

ANONYMOUS

FROM

The Horse of the Desert

~

. . . this matchless horse is the true pearl of every
        caravan;
The light and life of all our camps, – the force and glory
        of his clan.

~

TU FU

Protector-General Kao's Piebald Horse

TRANSLATED BY
Richard King

~

The Protector-General of Anhsi has a dark barbarian piebald
Of astonishing fame and value, which he has brought East.
As long as he has been fighting, this horse has been
      unequalled,
His mind at one with his master's, they have shared many
      triumphs.

After the triumphs he is cared for wherever they go
When he came from afar, from swirling winds and shifting
      sands,
Before his powerful frame had received the comforts of the
      stable,
His fierce heart was thinking again of glory to be won in
      battle.

His fetlocks are swift, his hoofs high and hard as iron,
A few steps on the Chao river and the thick ice cracked.
The five flowers quivered, clouds of steam rose from his
      body
Only after ten thousand li does the red sweat flow.

The strong men of Ch'ang-an dare not ride him,
The whole town knows he runs as fast as lightning.
Even when he wears a black silk halter, old in service of
      his master,
Will he not still long to be away on the road to the West?

~

WILL H. OGILVIE
Bridle Hand

~

This is a black of the rare old sort,
Deep through the heart and coupled short;
One of the kind our sires bestrode
When they took a jaunt on the Great North Road;
One of the type you might have seen
Carrying double to Gretna Green;
The type that a Turpin sat unstirred
When the roll of the London coach was heard.

Though the holsters never have round him hung,
Nor a Gretna bride to his pillion clung,
Though he never trots through the darkened oak,
Under mid-thigh boots and a riding cloak,
Or is reined in foam at the old inn door,
Where the guineas ring on the tap-room floor –
When the gallopers gather in hunting land
Where will you beat him, old Bridle Hand?

~

JOYCE WEST
The Station Hack

~

Not his the thrill of racing hooves and silken colours,
    He never heard the saddling paddock bell,

Nor from the crowded stand and rippling terrace
  The thunderous roars of acclamation swell.

Long days are his, the heat, and steady climbing,
  The narrow tracks behind the crawling sheep,
He hears the barking dogs, his master's whistle,
  The wind that blows across the lonely steep.

The bitter nights of early lambing weather,
  When storm darkness greys to sullen morn,
He breasts the angry streams, and on his saddle
  The weakling lamb is safely homeward borne.

The hills are his, the wide and lonely spaces
  That only winding bridle-pathways span,
And his the streams and good sweet homestead pastures –
  He is not servant, but the friend of man.

~

EDWARD PALMER
Norman the Stock-Horse
~

I have a friend – I've proved him so,
By many a task and token;
I've ridden him long and found him true,
Since first that he was broken.

For twenty years we both have been
In storm and sunny weather,
And many a thousand miles we've seen,
Just he and I together.

From Cooktown's breezy seaborn site,
By Palmer's golden river;
Where Mitchell's waters clear and bright,
Roll on their course for ever.

Across the Lynd and Gilbert's sands,
And many a rocky river;
Through trackless desert, forest lands,
We've journeyed oft together.

Then on the great grey plains so vast,
Where the sun's rays dance and quiver,
Through scorching heat and south-east blast,
We've toiled on Flinders River.

Through tangled scrubs and broken ground,
We have often had to scramble;
To wheel the cunning brumbies round,
From where they love to ramble.

Old Norman ne'er was known to fail,
Or in the camp to falter,

And just as sound today and hale,
As when he first wore halter.

Good horse, you well have earned your rest,
Your mustering days are over;
For all your time you'll have the best
And pass your life in clover.

The Indian's simple faith is plain,
That in the land of shadows
He'll have his faithful dog again
To hunt in misty meadows.

And should a steed a soul attain,
This surely then will follow –
I'll meet that grand old horse again,
And hail him 'Good old fellow!'

~

[241]

TU FU

A Barbarian Horse Owned by My Friend Mr Li from Hu-hsien

TRANSLATED BY
Richard King

~

My friend's fine horse is called Barbarian Bay.
A few years ago they fled from the bandit to Chin-niu.
They turned round and hurried back to see the Emperor,
He drank the water of the Han that morning, and was in
     Ling-chou by evening.

He boasts that Barbarian Bay is the finest horse of any
        age,
When they ride out, thousands and ten thousands envy
        him.
When I had fully heard of his strength in adversity,
I became increasingly sorry for other worn-out nags.

The sharp ears on his head prick up like autumn bamboo,
The high hoofs under his feet could cut frosted jade.
I realised then that dragon-horses are a breed apart,
Not to be compared with normal horses, that are so much
        worthless flesh.

Now the main road to Loyang is clear again
Day after day we enjoy ourselves and ride East together.
Horses with phoenix's heart and dragon's mane are not
        easily known,
With their bodies leaning forward, their eyes fixed, raising
        a strong wind.

~

[242]

WILL H. OGILVIE
The Arab Test
Sixty Miles a Day for Five Days
~

Since I have owned an Arab-bred
    And ridden him both fast and far
O'er many a Queensland watershed
    From rosy dawn to rising star,
By love of him my heart was led

To share with these the weary track
And step by step in fancy tread
　　Their daily journey out and back.

How well I know the lean game head,
　　The red fire smouldering in the eye,
The joyous plunge, the jaunty tread,
　　The courage that can never die;
The buoyant, bridle-slapping walk,
　　The loping canter long and clean,
The ear bent back to lover-talk
　　That passes man and horse between!

My heart went with them all the way –
　　Steel limbs, and bodies closely knit,
The tireless feet from day to day,
　　The firm necks arched against the bit,
The proud eyes blazing left and right,
　　The glinting of the dapple-stars,
The blown grey manes, the foam flecks white,
　　The lifting, dancing snaffle-bars!

In every breed man seeks the best,
　　And so this bitter task was theirs;
And who could braver face the test
　　Than offspring of the desert mares?
It matters not which steed was first,
　　Which kept his flesh, which did not tire, –
The dauntless courage of the worst
　　Has proved to all the Arab fire.

～

LORD BYRON

FROM

Mazeppa

~

'Bring forth the horse!' – the horse was brought;
  In truth, he was a noble steed,
  A Tartar of the Ukraine breed,
Who look'd as though the speed of thought
Were in his limbs; but he was wild,
  Wild as the wild deer, and untaught,
With spur and bridle undefiled –
  'Twas but a day he had been caught;
And snorting, with erected mane,
And struggling fiercely, but in vain,
In the full foam of wrath and dread
  To me the desert-born was led.

~

JAMES SHERIDAN KNOWLES

FROM
The Love Chase
Act II scene iii

~

What delight
To back the flying steed that challenges
The wind for speed! – seems native more of air
Than earth! – whose burden only lends him fire! –
Whose soul in his task, turns labour into sport!
Who makes your pastime his! I sit him now!
He takes away my breath! – He makes me reel!
I touch not earth – I see not – hear not – all
Is ecstasy of motion!

~

FINLAY McNAB
The Dun Mare

TRANSLATED BY
Thomas McLauchlan
AND ADAPTED BY
Grace Rhys

~

Gael-like is every leap of the dun mare,
A Gael she is in truth.
It is she who conquers and wins
In all that I'll now sing.

Men gather to praise her strength, –
She standing quiet by the house of prayer.
The birds of the wood alone.
Might match her in the race.
Just like the wheeling of the mountain winds
Is the action of the galloping mare,
Startling, rounded, bright, well-shod.
Gentle, broad-backed, coloured well.
Hundreds admire the spring of her
As like a mad thing, she goes by.
Like the point of an arrow, this horse;
Famous are all her doings.
That wave-like steed, hardy and keen,
Will win for her rider the praise of men.
Forth from her stall she takes the lead,
That gentle, great and active mare.
She will triumph in speed and slaughter
Till that the day in evening sinks.

≈

[246]

TU FU

A Painting of a Fine Horse from the Imperial Stables

TRANSLATED BY
Richard King

≈

I have heard the Emperor's horses could go a thousand li
  a day,
But none of the pictures of today are as fine as this one.

How martial and heroic are his will and bearing!
When he swishes his tail, it is like the North wind rising
      up.

His coat is dark and glossy, both his ears are yellow
His eyes gleam with a purple flame, the two pupils are
      square.
A spirit warlike as a dragon's uniting the flux of the
      universe,
A frame uniquely strong, opening out into a mighty
      gallop.

Formerly the herd-chief Chang Ching-hsun
Inspected the colts in all the herds to pick out the finest,
He ordered the stable-head to keep it in the Imperial
      Stables,
They reared the fine thoroughbred apart and loved it for
      its prowess.

At that time there were four hundred thousand horses,
Lord Chang was grieved that all were inferior to this one.
So he had this one alone portrayed for posterity.
Those who sit before it will think it fresh when it is old.

Many years have gone since the horse died, we have only
      the image,
Alas that his mighty strides can gallop no more!
Surely there must still be Yao-niao's and Hua-liu's today?
If the age has no Po Lo or Wang Liang, they die and are
      lost.

~

KAO SHIH
Lines on a Horse-Painting

TRANSLATED BY
Richard King

~

This fine horse from the stables of a Lord
Is depicted in a painting:

His hide has 'joined-cash' marking, his hoofs are the
      colour of iron,
In the sunlight of the painting, the tall horse has a jade
      bridle.
He runs but does not move, coming powerfully forward,
So swift his gallop that the dust is not stirred.

Moved by this exceptional painting, we praise the artist's
      sublime skill
But in discussing it, we cannot find sufficient words of
      praise.
The Ch'i-liu walked alone; this could be prized as high,
Why should one want to have ten thousand other nags?

For there will never be another like the fine horse from
      the stables.
Attached to an ornate chariot
He outpaces the flying swans;
He permits his master to groom him, his master to ride
      him,
And gallops a thousand li a day like a whirlwind.

~

TORQUATO TASSO

FROM

Jerusalem Delivered

Raymond's horse is described as being bred from the gale.

∼

   . . . Aquiline of matchless speed;
The banks of Tagus bred this generous steed:
There the fair mother of the warrior brood
(Soon as the kindly spring had fired her blood)
With open mouth, against the breezes held,
Receiv'd the gales with warmth prolific filled:
And (strange to tell) inspir'd with genial seed,
Her swelling womb produc'd this wondrous steed.
Along the sand with rapid feet he flies,
No eye his traces in the dust descries;
To right, to left, obedient to the rein,
He winds the mazes of th' embattled plain.

∼

ANONYMOUS

The Navajo Horse Story

TRANSLATED BY
Louis Watchman

~

My horse with a mane made of short rainbows.
My horse with ears of round corn.
My horse with eyes made of big stars.
My horse with a head made of mixed waters.
My horse with teeth made of white shell.
The long rainbow is in his mouth for a bridle
And with it I guide him.
When my horse neighs,
Different coloured horses follow.
When my horse neighs
Different coloured sheep follow.
I am wealthy because of him.
Before me peaceful
Behind me peaceful
Under me peaceful
Over me peaceful –
Peaceful voice when he neighs.
I am everlasting and peaceful
I stand for my horse.

~

TU FU

Staff-officer Fang's Barbarian Horse

TRANSLATED BY
Richard King

~

It is a barbarian horse of Ta-yuan breed,
Fine-boned and with a lean frame.
His ears pricked sharp as bamboo-shoots,
His four feet treat lightly and swift as the wind.

Wherever he goes, no open spaces defy him,
Fit to entrust life and death to.
When one has a fine horse like this,
One could travel ten thousand li with ease.

~

[251]

CALPURNIUS SICULUS

FROM

Eclogues vi

~

My beast displays
A deep-set back; a head and neck
That tossing proudly feel no check
From over-bulk; feet fashioned slight,
Thin flanks, and brow of massive height;
While in its narrow horny sheath
A well-turned hoof is bound beneath.

~

GUILLAUME DE SALLUSTE DU BARTAS

FROM

Treatise of the Handy-crafts
The fourth part of the first day of the second week

TRANSLATED BY
Joshua Sylvester

～

Cain as they say with his deep fear disturbed,
Then first of all the undaunted courser curbed;
That whilst about another's feet he run
With lusty speed, he might his death's-man shun.
Among a hundred brave, light, lusty Horses,
(With curious eye marking their curious forces)
He chooseth one for his industrious proof,
With round, high, hollow, smooth, brown, jetty hoof;
With pasterns short, upright, but yet in mean
Dry sinnowy shanks, strong, fleshless knees, and lean,
With hart-like legs, broad breast, and large behind,
With body large, smooth flanks, and double-chined;
A crested neck, bow'd like a half-bent bow,
Whereon a long thin curled Mane doth flow;
A firm full tail, touching the lowly ground,
With dock between two fair fat buttocks round.
A pricked ear that rests as little space
As his light foot; a lean, bare, bony face,
Thin joule, his head yet of a middle size,
Full lively flaming, sprightly rowling eyes;
Great foming mouth, hot fuming nostrils wide,
Of chestnut hair, his forehead starrifi'd:
Two milky feet, a feather on his breast,
Whom seven years old at the next grasse he guest.
  This comely Jennet gently first he wins,
And then to back him actively begins.

Steady and straight he sits, turning his fight
Still 'twixt the ears of his Palfrey light.
The chafed horse, such thrall is suffering,
Begins to snuffe, to snort, to leap, to fling;
And flying swift his fearful Rider makes,
Like some unskilful Lad that undertakes
To hold some Ship's Helm, whilst the headlong tyde
Carries away its vessell, and her guide;
Who near to drowned in the jaws of death,
Pale, fearful, shivering, faint, and out of breath,
A thousand times (to Heaven erected eyes)
Repents him of so bold an enterprise;
But sitting fast, lesse hurt than fear'd, Cain
Boldens himselfe, and his brave horse againe
Brings him to pace, from pacing to his trot,
From trot to gallop, after runs him out
In full career, and at his courage smiles,
In sitting still, he runs so many miles.

   His pace is faire and free, his trot is light
As Tigers course, or Swallowes nimble flight;
And his brave gallop seems as swift to go,
As Biscaine Dart, or shafts from Russian Bow.
. . .

   The wise wax't Rider not esteeming best,
To take too much now of his lusty beast;
Refrains his fury, then with learned wand,
The triple-corvet makes him understand;
With skilful voyce he gently cheares his pride,
And on his neck his flattring palme doth glide;
He stops him steady still, new breath to take,
And in the same path brings him softly back;
But th'angry Steed, rising and rearing proudly,
Striking the stones, stamping, and neighing lowdly;
Cals for the combat, plunges, leaps, and prances,
Besomes the path, with sparkling eyes he glances;
Champs on his burnished Bit, and gloriously
His nimble fetlocks lifteth belly-high;
All side-long jaunts, on either side he justles,
And's waving crest coragiously he bristles;

Making the gazers glad on every side
To give more roome unto his portly pride.
  Cain gently strokes him, and now sure in seat,
Ambitiously seeks still some fresher feat;
To be more famous, one while trots the Ring,
Another while he doth him backward bring;
Then of all fear he makes him lightly bound,
And to each hand to menage rightly round;
To stop, to turn, to caper, and to swim,
To dance, to leap, to hold up any limme;
And all so done, with time, grace, ordred skill,
As both had but one body and one will;
T'one for his art no little glory gaines,
T'other through practice by degrees attaines
Grace in his gallop, in his pace agility,
Lightnesse of head, and in his stop facility;
Strength in his leap, and stedfast menagings,
Aptnesse in all, and in his course new wings.

∼

[253]

WILLIAM SHAKESPEARE

FROM

Venus and Adonis

∼

Look, when a painter would surpass the life,
In limning out a well-proportion'd steed,
His art with nature's workmanship at strife,
As if the dead the living should exceed;
  So did this horse excel a common one
  In shape, in courage, colour, pace and bone.

Round-hoof'd, short-jointed, fetlocks shag and long,
Broad breast, full eye, small head, and nostril wide,
High crest, short ears, straight legs and passing strong,
Thin mane, thick tail, broad buttock, tender hide:
Look, what a horse should have he did not lack,
Save a proud rider on so proud a back.

~

[254]

XENOPHON
~

If one induces the horse
To assume that carriage
Which it would adopt
Of its own accord when displaying its beauty,
Then, one directs the horse
To appear joyous and magnificent,
Proud and remarkable
For having been ridden.

~

WILLIAM SHAKESPEARE

FROM

Hamlet
Act IV scene vii

~

I've seen myself, and served against, the French,
And they can well on horseback: but this gallant
Had witchcraft in it; he grew unto his seat;
And to such wondrous doing brought his horse,
As he had been incorpsed and demi-natured
With the brave beast.

~

[256]

PAM BROWN

~

Brooks too wide for our leaping
Hedges far too high,
Loads too heavy for our moving
Burdens too cumbersome for us to bear.
Distances far beyond journeying –
The horse gave us mastery.

~

ADAM LINDSAY GORDON

FROM

Ye Wearie Wayfarer
Fytte III

~

So the coward will dare on the gallant horse
What he never would dare alone,
Because he exults in a borrowed force,
And a hardihood not his own.

~

[258]

ANONYMOUS

To Ride or Not to Ride?

~

To ride or not to ride? that is the question;
Whether 'tis nobler in the mind to suffer
The jeers and scoffs of hare-brained jockies,
Or boldly mount the prancing steed,
And by advent'rous gallop end them?
To ride, to walk no more; and by a horse
Of stout abilities, to say we end
The heart-ache, and the thousand weary strides
The London Cockney takes, 'tis a consummation
Devoutly to be wished. To ride – to fall –
Perchance to break one's neck; aye, there's the rub,
For in that ride what various ills may come,
When we have trotted on some few score miles,

Must give us pause – there's the respect
That makes the unwilling walker bear
The painful toil of padding all his life.
For who would bear the whips and taunts of coachmen,
The horse-dealer's wrong, the jockey's contumely,
The jokes of country girls, the buck's assurance,
The insolence of chairmen, and the spurns
Of brawny porters in the crowded streets,
When he himself might his quietus make
Upon a gentle pony? who would fardels bear,
To groan and sweat under a heavy load?
But that the dread of ev'ry untried horse,
Whose undiscovered humours and whose tricks
No traveller returns well pleased to tell,
And makes us rather walk in clouted shoes
Than fly to horses that we know not of.
Thus horror does make cowards of us all;
And thus the resolution of our riding
Is sicklied o'er with the pale cast of fear,
And beaux and cits, of genteel life and taste,
With this regard, from Tattersall's turn away,
And lose the name of horsemen.

~

G. A. FOTHERGILL

Bucking Sally

To Bt.-Colonel P. J. V. Kelly, C.M.G.,
D.S.O., 3rd (King's Own) Hussars (Temp.
Brig.-General in Palestine)

'Any steed that can loosen his rider's back teeth is said to be a real good bucker.' 'Sally', an imported broncho, was one of this order, and no mistake – oh, the 'hurricane deck' of that mare! All went the same way off her – each met his 'Waterloo'. Even the best rough-riding sergeant-major at Aldershot was shot off her and laid up for a week afterwards.

~

I sat on the back of a good-looking bay,
    So perfect in mouth and so moral, –
I *thought* so at least till the end of the day,
    When I'd ample excuse for a quarrel.

Not a horse of a hundred I knew in the place
    That had carried me over the Valley
Had ever quite thrown me in school or in chase
    Save this one, the bad bucking Sally.

(Pig-jumping is common in barracks and school,
    But bucking – bad bucking, uncommon);
And scarce had she offered to make me a fool
    When I knew I was leaving a rum 'un:

I had had my fun on the star of your stud,
    And we'd just about come to the Valley –
A plunge, a buck, another, then – thud!
    And I said good-bye to your Sally.

~

TU FU

Two Poems Given in Jest to Friends

TRANSLATED BY
Richard King

~

I

In the fourth month of the first year,
One of the secretaries, Editor Chiao,
Boasted that he was strong enough
To ride any colt, however lively.
One morning he was thrown and kicked,
His lip was torn, his front teeth smashed,
But his bold heart is undaunted,
He wants to go East to hunt Barbarians.

2

In the fourth month of the first year,
One of the officials, Inspector Wang,
Broke his left arm when his horse shied.
The bone was broken, his face blackened,
The wretched beast has floundered in deep mud.
Why did he not avoid the rainy weather?
But I exhort you, Sir, not to resent it;
You never know, it may well work out right . . .

~

LES MURRAY
The Lieutenant of Horse Artillery
~

Full tilt for my Emperor and King, I
galloped down the moonlit roads of Hungary
past poplar after Lombardy poplar tree
in our dear multicultural Empi-

re alas! on a horse I didn't know
had been requisitioned from a circus. Without fail
he leaped every tree-shadow lying like a fox's tail
over the road, O despite whip, despite Whoa!

unswerving, he hurdled them. My leather shako jerked,
my holster slapped my hip, my despatch case too,
every leap! I was clubbed black and blue
inside my tight trousers. So many shadows lurked

to make him soar and me cry out, taking wing
every fifty metres the length of a desperate ride
for my Emperor and King, as our Empire died
with its dream of happy cultures dancing in a ring.

~

WILL H. OGILVIE

The Master Horseman

~

His name I have lost in the lapse of the years –
   That man from Kentucky who came to the West
To challenge a round with the pitching Pin-Ears
   Who had baffled the bravest and beaten the best.

That dip in the Rockies I see in my dreams –
   The stir in the township; the crowd by the rails;
The men from the *mesa* with buggies and teams;
   The cowboys come in from the White River trails.

I remember the roping, the saddling, the cinching;
   The wrestling; the ramping; the dust round his feet;
The brown hand that reached for the horn without
      flinching;
   The light form that swung to that dangerous seat.

And I've seen a few buckers tuck heads, in my time;
   Raw colts on the Roper, old rogues on the Bree;
But I never saw one that could sunfish and climb
   Like that pointy-eared bay when his blinds were set
      free.

But the lad from the bluegrass sat straight as a lance,
   He raked him and fanned him all lathered in foam,
Then slipped from the saddle, slow smile in his glance,
   With a '*Yip! Colorado! – We've worse ones at home!*'

At dawn the next morning while hoofs scattered sand
   Where he faced the South trail with the packhorse he led,
As I spoke some rough praise he reached down for my
      hand,
   And '*I sure HAD to ride him!*' was all that he said.

I have travelled a bit and I've seen some good men,
    But it's once in a lifetime the Master occurs,
And I know, though I never shall see him again,
    That here was a horseman 'from Stetson to spurs'!

~

[263]

WILLIAM SHAKESPEARE

FROM

King Henry IV part I
Act IV scene i

~

I saw young Harry, with his beaver on,
His cuisses on his thighs, gallantly arm'd,
Rise from the ground like feather'd Mercury,
And vaulted with such ease into his seat,
As if an angel dropp'd down from the clouds,
To turn and wind a fiery Pegasus
And witch the world with noble horsemanship.

~

ANONYMOUS

FROM

Sir Gawain and the Green Knight

This poem was written in the last quarter of the fourteenth
century, in the reign of Richard II. We do not know the writer's
name or anything about him. The poem is a perfect piece of
artistry, written in Middle English.

In the following extract 'blonk' means 'horse', thonk=thank,
wlonk=lovely, burne= warrior, snaped= pinched,
werbeland=whistling.

~

Now nighs the New Year, and the night passes,
The dawn drives at the dark, as the dear God bids;
But wild weathers of the world wakened therefrom,
Clouds cast keenly the cold to the earth,
Bitter the North blew, the naked to bite;
The snow snitered full snart, and snaped the wild.
The werbeland wind wapped from on high,
And drove each dale full of drifts full great.
The lord listened full well as he lay in his bed,
Though he locked his lids full little he slept;
By each cock that crew he knew well the steven,
Stepped swift from his bed ere the day sprang,
By the light of a lamp that lit up his chamber;
He spoke to his squire who swiftly him answered,
And bade him bring him his byrnie and his blonk saddle.
First he clad him in his clothes to ward off the cold
And then his other harness that had holdly been kept,
Both his paunce and his plates, polished full clean,
The rust rubbed from the rings of his rich byrnie
And all was fresh as at first, and he was fain then to
          thonk;
     He had upon each piece,
     Wiped full well and wlonk;

The gayest unto Grece,
The burne bade bring his blonk.

~

[265]

ANEURIN

The Lovely Youth

TRANSLATED BY
H. Idris Bell

~

The youth had a man's heart; he was a man in the din of
       battle.
Horses, swift and thick-maned, bore the lovely youth.
A light broad shield on flanks thin and fleet.
Swords blue and bright, golden spurs and fine cloth.
No hatred shall there be between thee and me;
better will I do with thee, to praise thee in song.
Sooner will his blood be spent than he go to the wedding
       feast;
Sooner to be food for ravens than to the funeral rites.

~

ADAM LINDSAY GORDON

FROM

The Roll of the Kettledrum or, The Lay of the Last Charger

~

It may be, – we follow, and though we inherit
Our strength for a season, our pride for a span,
Say! vanity are they? vexation of spirit?
Not so, since they serve for a time horse and man.

They serve for a time, and they make life worth living,
In spite of life's troubles – 'tis vain to despond;
Oh, man! *we* at least, *we* enjoy, with thanksgiving,
God's gifts on this earth, though we look not beyond.

You sin, and *you* suffer, and we, too, find sorrow,
Perchance through *your* sin – yet it soon will be o'er;
We labour today, and we slumber tomorrow,
Strong horse and bold rider! – and *who knoweth more?*

~

LIONEL JOHNSON

FROM

By the Statue of King Charles at Charing Cross

~

Comely and calm, he rides
Hard by his own Whitehall:
Only the night wind glides:
No crowds, nor rebels, brawl.

Gone, too, his Court: and yet,
The stars his courtiers are:
Stars in their stations set;
And every wandering star.

Alone he rides, alone,
The fair and fatal King:
Dark night is all his own,
That strange and solemn thing.

. . .

Armoured he rides, his head
Bare to the stars of doom:
He triumphs now, the dead,
Beholding London's gloom.

. . .

King, tried in fires of woe!
Men hunger for thy grace:
And through the night I go,
Loving thy mournful face.

~

W. K. HOLMES

FROM

Jimmy – Killed in Action

~

Horses he loved, and laughter, and the sun,
A song, wide spaces and the open air;
The trust of all dumb living things he won,
And never knew the luck too good to share.

. . .

Now, though he will not ride with us again,
His merry spirit seems our comrade yet,
Freed from the power of weariness and pain,
Forbidding us to mourn – or to forget.

~

W. B. YEATS

FROM

Under Ben Bulben

~

Under bare Ben Bulben's head
In Drumcliff churchyard Yeats is laid . . .
On limestone quarried near the spot
By his command these words are cut:
     Cast a cold eye
     On life, on death.
     Horseman, pass by!

~

RUDYARD KIPLING
The Undertaker's Horse

To-tschin-shu is condemned to death. How can he drink tea with
the Executioner? *Japanese Proverb*.

~

The eldest son bestrides him,
And the pretty daughter rides him,
And I meet him oft o' mornings on the Course;
And there wakens in my bosom
An emotion chill and gruesome
As I canter past the Undertaker's Horse.

Neither shies he nor is restive,
But a hideously suggestive
Trot, professional and placid, he affects:
And the cadence of his hoof-beats
To my mind this grim reproof beats:
'Mend your pace, my friend, I'm coming. Who's the
          next?'

Ah! stud-bred of ill-omen,
I have watched the strongest go – men
Of pith and might and muscle – at your heels,
Down the plantain-bordered highway,
(Heaven send it ne'er be my way!)
In a lacquered box and jetty upon wheels.

Answer, sombre beast and dreary,
Where is Brown, the young, the cheery,
Smith, the pride of all his friends and half the Force?
You were at that last dread *dak*
We must cover at a walk,
Bring them back to me, O Undertaker's Horse!

With your mane unhogged and flowing,
And your curious way of going,
And that business-like black crimping of your tail,
E'en with Beauty on your back, Sir,
Pacing as a lady's hack, Sir,
What wonder when I meet you I turn pale?

It may be you wait your time, Beast,
Till I write my last bad rhyme, Beast,
Quit the sunlight, cut the rhyming, drop the glass,
Follow after with the others,
Where some dusky heathen smothers
Us with marigolds in lieu of English grass.

Or, perchance, in years to follow,
I shall watch your plump sides hollow,
See Carnifex (gone lame) become a corse,
See old age at last o'erpower you,
And the Station Pack devour you,
I shall chuckle then, O Undertaker's Horse!

But to insult, jibe, and quest, I've
Still the hideously suggestive
Trot that hammers out the grim and warning text,
And I hear it hard behind me
In what place soe'er I find me:
'Sure to catch you sooner or later. Who's the next?'

ANONYMOUS

FROM

Story of the Trojan War

Xanthus, the Horse, speaks, and predicts his master's death
(Achilles).

~

Yes, great Achilles, we this day again
Will bear thee safely; but thy hour of doom
Is nigh at hand; nor shall we cause thy death,
But Heav'n's high will, and Fate's imperious pow'r.
By no default of ours, nor lack of speed,
The Trojans stripp'd Patroclus of his arms:
The mighty god, fair-hair'd Latona's son,
Achiev'd his death, and Hector's vict'ry gained.
Our speed of foot may vie with Zephyr's breeze,
Deem'd swiftest of the winds; but thou art doom'd
To die, by force combin'd of god and man.

~

HENRY WADSWORTH LONGFELLOW

FROM

Burial of the Minnisink

The burial of a Red Indian Chief.

~

Before, a dark-haired virgin train
Chanted the death dirge of the slain;
Behind, the long procession came
Of hoary men and chiefs of fame,
With heavy hearts, and eyes of grief,
Leading the war-horse of their chief.

Stripped of his proud and martial dress,
Uncurbed, unreined, and riderless,
With darting eye, and nostril spread,
And heavy and impatient tread,
He came; and oft that eye so proud
Asked for his rider in the crowd.

They buried the dark chief; they freed
Beside the grave his battle steed;
And swift an arrow cleaved its way
To his stern heart! One piercing neigh
Arose, and, on the dead man's plain,
The rider grasps his steed again.

~

MATTHEW ARNOLD

FROM

Sohrab and Rustum

~

. . . and Ruksh, the horse,
Who stood at hand, utter'd a dreadful cry:
No horse's cry was that, most like the roar
Of some pain'd desert lion, who all day
Hath trail'd the hunter's javelin in his side,
And comes at night to die upon the sand.

~

[274]

PERCY BYSSHE SHELLEY

FROM

The Revolt of Islam

~

Was there a human spirit in the steed
That thus with his proud voice, ere night was gone,
He broke our linkèd rest? or do indeed
All living things a common nature own,
And thought erect a universal throne,
Where many shapes one tribute ever bear?
And Earth, their mutual mother, does she groan
To see her sons contend? And makes she bare
Her breast, that all in peace its drainless stores may share?

~

SIR WALTER SCOTT

FROM

The Death of Keeldar

From a true story of Percival Rede of Trochend, in Redesdale.

～

Up rose the sun o'er moor and mead;
Up with the sun rose Percy Rede;
Brave Keeldar, from his couples freed,
    Career'd along the lea;
The palfry sprung with sprightly bound,
As if to match the gamesome hound;
His horn the gallant huntsman wound;
    They were a jovial three!

Man, hound, or horse, of higher fame,
To wake the wild deer never came,
Since Alnwick's Earl pursued the game
    On Cheviot's rueful day;
Keeldar was matchless in his speed,
Than Tarras, ne'er was stauncher steed,
A peerless archer, Percy Rede:
    And right dear friends were they.

. . .

Dilated nostrils, staring eyes,
Mark the poor palfrey's mute surprise,
He knows not that his comrade dies,
    Nor what is death – but still
His aspect hath expression drear
Of grief and wonder, mix'd with fear,
Like startled children when they hear
    Some mystic tale of ill.

～

THOMAS BABINGTON MACAULAY

FROM

Lays of Ancient Rome
The Battle of Lake Regillus

~

Fast, fast, with heels and wild spurning,
The dark-grey charger fled:
He burst through ranks of fighting men;
He sprang o'er heaps of dead.
His bridle far out-streaming,
His flanks all blood and foam,
He sought the southern mountains,
The mountains of his home.
The pass was steep and rugged,
The wolves they howled and whined;
But he ran like a whirlwind up the pass,
And he left the wolves behind.
Through many a startled hamlet
Thundered his flying feet;
He rushed through the gate of Tusculum,
He rushed up the long white street;
He rushed by tower and temple,
And paused not from his race
Till he stood before his master's door
In the stately market-place.
And straightway round him gathered
A pale and trembling crowd,
And when they knew him, cries of rage
Brake forth, and wailing loud:
And women rent their tresses
For their great prince's fall;
And old men girt on their old swords,
And went to man the wall.

But, like a graven image,
Black Auster kept his place,
And ever wistfully he looked
Into his master's face.
The raven-mane that daily,
With pats and fond caresses,
The young Herminia washed and combed
And twined in even tresses,
And decked with coloured ribands
From her own gay attire,
Hung sadly o'er her father's corpse
In carnage and in mire.

≈

[277]

ANONYMOUS

FROM

The Lay of Sir Grue'lan

TRANSLATED BY
G. L. Way

From the Fabliaux, short French verse tales of the twelfth and
thirteenth centuries.

≈

But for the palfrey Gedefer, who stood
Reft of his lord beside that wondrous flood,
As with his loss distraught the peerless steed
Spurned the green sward, and madly scoured the mead;
Shrill doleful neighing night and day were heard,
And still amain he fled when man appeared.
So passed his life. E'en now, tradition holds,
Oft as that day the circling year unfolds,

By the stream side is seen the steed forlorn,
And for his fruitless search is heard to mourn.
Soon through the land the dittied story spread
Of the good knight and of his faithful steed;
And some choice mind, in rhyme's propitious day,
From the rude strain wrought out Grue'lan's lay.

~

EDWIN GERARD
The Horse That Died for Me
~

They gave me a fiery horse to groom, and I rode him on
      parade,
While he plunged and swung for kicking room like a
      young and haughty jade.
I rode him hard till I curbed his will, hot-foot in the sham
      attack,
Till he ceased to jib, and took to drill like a first-class
      trooper's hack.

He tasted hell on the Indian Sea; pent up in the gloom
      below,
He dreamed of the days when he was free, and his weary
      heart beat slow.
But he lived to leave the reeking ship, and he raised his
      drooping head
With new-born zest when he felt the grip of earth beneath
      his tread.

I left him and sailed away to fight on foot in the trenches
        deep –
A stretch that passed like an awful hour of fearsome
        nightmare sleep.
I lived to search for a mount once more on the crowded
        piquet line:
I rode him out as I did before, when I'd claimed the horse
        as mine.

I loved him as only one who knows the way of a horse may
        love;
Who rides athirst when the hell-wind blows and the sun
        stands still above;
Who rides for cover behind the rise that lifts like a wall of
        woe
And smites the vision of burning eyes when the Moslem lead
        rips low.

Far out on the hock-deep sands that roll in waves to the
        flaming sky,
He carried me far on the night patrol where the Turkish
        outposts lie;
He took me back to the camp at noon when the skirmish died
        amain,
And under a white and spectral moon he bore me afield again.

Our squadrons surged to the left and right when the fire of
        day was dead;
The foemen crept in the sombre night with a wary, noiseless
        tread.
We moved away on a flanking march, like a brown line
        rudely drawn
That reached the foot of the grey sky's arch in the waking
        light of dawn.

The line closed in when the red sun shot from the purple-
        tinted east
To glare with scorn on the wretched lot of man and his jaded
        beast.

I urged my horse with a purpose grim for a ridge where
    cover lay,
And my heart beat high for the heart of him when he
    saved my life that day.

His knees gave way and I slipped from him: he dropped
    in a sprawling heap
On the wind-gapped edge of the skyline's rim where the
    high-blown sand was deep;
And fear came down with a gusty rain of lead on his final
    bed . . .
Before I turned for cover again I knew that his life had
    fled.

My heart is warm for a heart that died in the desert flank
    attack,
And the white sand surges down to hide the bones of a
    trooper's hack.

~

[279]

P. G. R. BENSON
The End
~

Gentle caress of a muzzle,
  Soft little whimpering neigh!
Stronger than words to awaken
  Memory's wondrous array.

Measures can fathom the ocean,
  Reckon the swiftness of light;

Where is the standard for sorrow?
   Where is the standard for right?

Where is the meter of sadness
   Gauging the grief of good-bye
Bid to a favourite hunter?
   What is the depth of a sigh?

Standards of measure are futile,
   Vain is the effort to tell;
Only the one who has felt it
   Plumbs the full depth of farewell.

One loving pat in the stable,
   One little catch at the heart,
One little sorrowing silent
   Kiss of two spirits that part.

~

[280]

JOHN ORR EWING

Dandy

~

He lies at rest beneath the shade
Of trees on Brooksby lawn,
The horse that led the Light Brigade
That fateful winter's morn.

They say that here on All Soul's Eve
Those phantom squadrons pass –
What patterns strange their shadows weave
Across the moonlit grass! –

Lord Cardigan, their leader, sits
On 'Dandy' at their head,
You even hear the chink of bits,
And hoof-beats of the dead.

The moon goes in: the shadows fade.
The night is dark again.
The heroes of the Light Brigade
Return beyond our ken.

What proof have we that such things be?
The answer must be, 'none':
Yet things exist we cannot see,
Why should not this be one?

~

[281]

R. E. EGERTON WARBURTON
The Dead Hunter
~

His sire from the desert, his dam from the north,
The pride of my stable stepped gallantly forth,
One slip in his stride as the scurry he led,
And my steed, ere his rivals o'ertook him, lay dead.

Poor steed! shall thy limbs on the hunting field lie,
That his beak in thy carcass the raven may die?
Is it thine the sad doom of thy race to fulfil,
Thy flesh to the cauldron, thy bones to the mill?

Ah no! – I behold thee a foal yet unshod,
Now race round the paddock, now roll on the sod;

Where first thy young hoof the green herbage impressed,
There, the shoes on thy feet, will I lay thee to rest!

~

[282]

G. J. WHYTE-MELVILLE

FROM

*The Place where the
Old Horse Died*

~

There are men both good and wise who hold that in a
        future state
Dumb creatures we have cherished here below
Shall give us glorious greeting when we pass the golden
        gate;
Is it folly that I hope it may be so?
For never man had friend
More enduring to the end,
Truer mate in turn of time and tide.
Could I think we'd meet again
It would lighten half my pain
At the place where the old horse died.

~

EMPEROR HADRIAN

Epitaph on his Favourite Horse

TRANSLATED BY
J. Wight Duff and Arnold M. Duff

~

Borysthenes the Alan
Was mighty Caesar's steed:
O'er marshland and o'er level,
O'er Tuscan Hills, with speed
He used to fly . . .
The foam from off his lips,
As oft may chance, would sprinkle
His tail e'en to the tips.
But he in youthful vigour,
His limbs unsapped by toil,
On his own day extinguished,
Here lies beneath the soil.

~

ANONYMOUS

Anonymi Speudeusa Equae Epitaphium

TRANSLATED BY
R. E. and O. Way

This fourth-century epitaph is one of the earliest examples of rhymed Latin verse. In translation it is almost impossible to render the superbly epigrammatic quality of the original.

~

Gaetula harena prosata
Gaetulo equino consita
Cursando Flabis compara
Aetate abacta virginis
Speudeusa Lethen incolis.

Stretched on the Barbary sand you lie
By a Barbary's covering doomed to die,
Speudeusa – like the winds that fly.
De-flowered mare, no longer maid,
You must inhabit Lethe's shade.

~

PENNY RADCLYFFE

The Dead Foal

～

She started foaling late at night,
The foal half born was dead, stuck fast.
I left to call the vet; she neighed
'Don't leave me!' 'I'll be back,' I said.
The foal at last removed, lay wet,
Its tongue out, mouth wide open,
Legs half twisted and deformed.
'Just leave her with it,' said the vet,
'And she'll stay quiet then,' and so I did.
Later I offered her a warm bran feed,
She laid her ears back when I neared
And moved between me and her child.
Licked it, then with lifted fore foot
Pushed it gently and bit its cold wet hide.
She did not understand.
Six foals she'd borne before
And all had risen quickly after birth,
Followed her and suckled at her teats.
All day she stood beside her stiffened child,
Her head hung low and grieving without tears.
At night she wandered off to graze.
We took the foal away,
She raised her head and neighed
Then started cropping grass again.
Her grief, as sharp as any human grief, was over now.

～

BIOGRAPHICAL
INDEX OF POETS

References are to poem numbers.

CLAUDE COLEER ABBOTT (1889–1971) 108
First world war poet, a second lieutenant in the Irish Guards.
Later Professor of English at the University of Durham, he visited
and lectured in the USA on several occasions.

ANEURIN (late sixth – early seventh century) 265
Welsh poet, best known for the *Gododin*, a celebration of a battle
fought in 603.

ANONYMOUS 2, 20, 21, 49, 52, 57, 64, 65, 68, 77, 78, 91, 133,
138, 162, 222, 236, 249, 258, 264, 271, 277, 284

MATTHEW ARNOLD (1822–88) 46, 66, 273
Poet and critic, educated at Rugby (where his father was head-
master) and Oxford. Private Secretary to Lord Lansdowne and an
Inspector of Schools.

UNA AULD 10
Poet and writer of romantic novels from New Zealand, published
in the 1960s.

P. G. R. BENSON 137, 279
Writing before the first world war, privately published poet.

JOHN BETJEMAN (1906–84) 226
Educated at Marlborough and Magdalene College Oxford. Wrote
about the contemporary scene, and encouraged interest in Victor-
ian architecture. Poet Laureate.

THE BIBLE 55, 69

WILLIAM BLAKE (1757–1827) 129
Poet and engraver, he did not receive a normal school education
but was brought up amongst much reading of treatises on
Gnosticism and Druidism.

WILFRID SCAWEN BLUNT (1840–1922) 178, 185
Poet and publicist, served in the diplomatic service 1858–70.
Together with his wife, Lady Anne, he bred Arab horses at
Crabbet Park, one of the finest studs in the country and of lasting
influence.

ALISON BRACKENBURY (b. 1953) 23, 38, 48, 112, 155, 200,
204, 231, 235
Born in Lincolnshire, living in Gloucestershire with two old but
lively ponies. Has published some books of poetry, and her poems
have also appeared in *The Spectator* and been heard on BBC
Radio 4.

G. A. BRANT 50
US horseman.

PAM BROWN (b. 1928) 256
A wartime evacuee, after training in dance and art she made an
abortive attempt to sail round the world. A varied life with an
interest in boats led to publication in that subject and to
commissions for poems and an LCC poetry prize.

ROBERT BROWNING (1812–89) 168, 210
Fine and prolific Victorian poet, born in Camberwell, Surrey. He
was an avid reader from childhood and a keen musician. His
second home was Italy.

SIR MICHAEL WILLIAM SELBY BRUCE (b. 1894) 219
Baronet of Stenhouse. In his autobiography he describes himself
as 'a man who had fled convention, as a policeman in Rhodesia, a
soldier in the war, a sailor before the mast, a cowboy, a journalist,
a rancher, a schoolmaster, a big game hunter, an explorer, an
engineer, a surveyor and a film actor'.

GEORGE GORDON, LORD BYRON (1788–1824) 62, 243
Poet, born in London, his father died when he was three and he
was brought up in difficult circumstances, not helped by being
lame. Educated at Harrow and Trinity College Cambridge, he
eventually succeeded to his great-uncle's title and estates. He
spent much of his life abroad and involved himself in the Greek
struggle for liberation from Turkey.

TITUS CALPURNIUS SICULUS (first century) 251
Latin pastoral poet, much influenced by Virgil.

DAVID CAMPBELL (b. 1911) 93
Born New South Wales, educated at King's School, Sydney and
Cambridge University. He was a keen athlete. Returned to
Australia in 1938 and joined the RAAF at the outbreak of war.

ROY CAMPBELL (1902–57) 72
South African writer, he lived most of his life in England and
Europe. He fought in the Spanish Civil War and in the British
Army in the second world war. Killed in a car crash in Portugal.

THOMAS CAMPBELL (1777–1844) 15
Scottish poet who originally studied law but then settled for a
literary life. Possibly his best-known poem is 'The Battle of the
Baltic'.

GEOFFREY CHAUCER (c. 1345–1400) 181
Born in London and connected in an official capacity to the royal
court. The father of English poetry.

FRANCES CORNFORD (1886–1960) 101
The granddaughter of Charles Darwin and a friend of the poet
Rupert Brooke.

PETER CORNISH (b. 1929) 113, 119
Educated at St Catherine's College Cambridge and was for many
years a university teacher. He now lives in Newmarket and works
with horses, with whom he has a natural rapport and a deep
understanding.

BARRY CORNWALL, see PROCTER

JOHN COVERNTON 71
Writing in Libya in 1944.

WILLIAM COWPER (1731–1800) 208
Son of a rector and descended through his mother from the poet
John Donne. 'The Task' is thought to be his greatest work.

'DALESMAN' 176
The pseudonym of a writer in *Horse and Hound*.

'DASHWOOD' 191
The pseudonym of a writer in *The New Sporting Magazine* in the
early nineteenth century.

WILLIAM BROMLEY DAVENPORT (1821–1884) 194
A keen fieldsportsman.

THOMAS DE GREY (fl. 1639) 223
Author of *The Compleat Horse-man and Expert Ferrier*.

WALTER DE LA MARE (1873–1956) 89
Born of Huguenot stock in Kent and educated at St Paul's
Cathedral Choir School. Poet and novelist for both adults and
children.

SID DELANY 96
Modern Australian writer.

CHARLES DIBDEN (1745–1814) 130
Born in Southampton, he was variously a singer, actor and
composer of stage music, and achieved fame as a song writer.

ROBERT DODSLEY (1703–1764) 146
Poet, dramatist and bookseller. Wrote several plays well thought
of in their day, some of which were performed at Covent Garden.

SIR ARTHUR CONAN DOYLE (1859–1930) 186
Born in Edinburgh, he was a qualified medical practitioner and
writer of many books including the Sherlock Holmes stories.

SIR FRANCIS HASTINGS DOYLE (1810–88) 164
Professor of Poetry at Oxford, 1867–77.

GUILLAUME DE SALLUSTE DU BARTAS (1544–90) 221, 252
French poet. Widely read in his time, mostly for his works on the creation of the world. This was translated into rhymed decasyllabic couplets by Joshua Sylvester (1563–1618).

RONALD DUNCAN (b. 1914) 53
Playwright and librettist, and breeder of Arab horses.

JOHN ORR EWING 124, 141, 144, 188, 280
Major and holder of the MC, his poems are inspired by the countryside and a typical English life. He hunted in the shires and wrote many poems of his experiences between the wars.

ELEANOR FARJEON (1881–1965) 35
Daughter of an English novelist, she is well known for her children's stories and poems.

G. A. FOTHERGILL (1868–1945) 36, 60, 94, 114, 165, 259
Artist and writer, mainly on the subject of horses and hunting. He was a surgeon in the 1st Cavalry Brigade during the first world war and was a painter and water colourist of some merit.

ROBERT FROST (1874–1963) 9, 206
Born in San Francisco, his poetry is mainly about New England where he spent most of his life. Winner of the Pulitzer Prize three times, he received honorary doctorates from both Oxford and Cambridge.

CHRISTOPHER FRY (b. 1907) 88
Born in Bristol, his father, an Anglican Lay preacher, died when he was three years old. He became an actor and the rest of his career was connected with the theatre, as actor, producer, director and playwright.

EDWIN GERARD (1891–1965) 278
Born in South Australia. Served with the Light Horse in Palestine in the first world war, and then became a poet and farmer. Wrote many ballads under the pseudonym of 'Trooper Gerardy'.

ADAM LINDSAY GORDON (1833–70) 140, 166, 175, 180, 257, 266

The son of an Army officer, he started life as an army cadet but then emigrated to Australia in 1853. He was at various times a mounted policeman, horse-trainer, and member of the Australian Parliament, and he achieved some success as a steeplechase rider and a poet. Debts and injuries led him to shoot himself.

JULIAN GRENFELL (1888–1915) 56
Eldest son of Lord Desborough. Soldier poet, killed in action and awarded the DSO. 'Into Battle' is thought to be his finest poem.

GWERFYL MECHAIN (fl. 1462–1500) 230
Described as 'the Welsh Sappho'. Not much is known about her, but she lived in Powys and may have been a tavern keeper.

EMPEROR HADRIAN (76–138) 283
Roman emperor, known for his great journey all over Europe and the Middle East. Builder of Hadrian's wall. A just ruler and lover of the arts.

JOSEPH HALL (1574–1656) 158
Bishop of Exeter and Norwich, suspected of Puritanism and spent time in the Tower of London before being deprived of his living.

SIR GEORGE ROSTREVOR HAMILTON (1888–1967) 8
Poet, writer and civil servant, educated at Exeter College Oxford. A classics scholar and commissioner for taxes.

A. M. HARBORD 34
English army officer, writing between the wars.

THOMAS HARDY (1840–1928) 103
From a rather poor family, he was a prolific novelist and poet and wrote much about his native West Country.

A. P. HERBERT (1890–1971) 150
Writer and politician, called to the bar but did not practise law. Wrote for *Punch* and was one of the outstanding wits of his generation.

W. K. HOLMES 123, 268
A first world war poet from Scotland.

HOMER (ninth century BC) 16, 67, 76, 148
Greek epic poet. His most famous translator into English was
George Chapman, who published both the *Iliad* and the *Odyssey* in
1616. Several other poets followed with translations through the
centuries, those of Alexander Pope being another significant body
of work.

GERARD MANLEY HOPKINS (1844–89) 220
Known as the first of the Modern Poets, though born a Victorian.
He became a Jesuit priest and was said to have 'a poet's pen, a
painter's eye and a musician's ear'.

PATRICK HORE-RUTHVEN 27
Australian, in the Rifle Brigade in North Africa in the second
world war. He became a Captain in a commando unit and was
killed in Tripolitania in 1942.

LAURENCE HOUSMAN (1865–1959) 75
Younger brother of the poet A.E. Famous as an artist and
illustrator, but also wrote poetry, plays and fiction.

WILFRED HOWE-NURSE 106
English poet writing during the first world war and later.

TED HUGHES (b. 1930) 87
Born in Yorkshire, educated at Pembroke College Cambridge.
Poet Laureate.

JACK HURLBURT 31
American horseman, farrier, veterinary practitioner and judge.

ROBIN IVY (b. 1919) 25, 85, 153, 182
Born in Bedford, a keen naturalist and animal lover who has
published several poems. He spent time with horses in his teens,
when his parents were in the Far East, and has hunted with the
Croome.

LIONEL JOHNSON (1867–1902) 267
Poet and critic..It is said of his poem 'By the Statue of King
Charles' that there is no better poem of a 'lost cause'.

FERENC JUHÁSZ (b. 1928) 3
Hungarian writer from a peasant background. He worked as an agricultural labourer and factory worker before going into publishing and writing.

KAO SHIH (seventh – eighth century) 247
Born in poverty in China, he wrote operatic pieces for a travelling theatre before becoming a secretary and then a soldier. Turned to poetry in his old age.

FRANK KENDON (1893–1959) 5
Poet and Fellow of St John's College Cambridge.

CHARLES KINGSLEY (1819–1875) 173
A student of King's College London and Magdalene College Cambridge. He was Professor of Modern History at Cambridge, an ordained clergyman, and very involved in Christian Socialism. He is best known for his prose and stories such as *The Water Babies*.

RUDYARD KIPLING (1865–1936) 30, 90, 171, 229, 270
Born in Bombay. His father was the curator of the Lahore Museum with interests in several arts. He was educated in England at the United Services' College in Devonshire, but returned to India in 1882 to become a journalist. He wrote many novels, poems and children's stories, mainly about India.

JAMES SHERIDAN KNOWLES (1784–1862) 244
Born in Cork, Ireland, he was at various times a doctor, playwright, soldier, actor and lecturer.

THE KORAN 51, 63, 213
The Moslem scriptures.

THOMAS KYD (1558–1594) 7
Best known for his play *The Spanish Tragedy*. He was imprisoned for atheism in 1593 and died in poverty.

E. LADSON 211
Published in *Pony* magazine.

PHILIP LARKIN (1922–85) 120
Born in Coventry, educated at St John's College Oxford. Poet and novelist, about whom much has been written.

D. H. LAWRENCE (1885–1930) 24
He wrote some fine poems, but is best known for his novels about English life.

FELIX LEAKEY (b. 1922) 125, 179, 189, 197, 215
Emeritus Professor of French in the University of London. He has written poetry all his life, but especially since his retirement to Northumberland in 1985. A keen hunting man, he has hunted in many parts of England as well as in Scotland, Ireland and France.

MAURICE LINDSAY (b. 1918) 207
A Scottish editor, anthologist and author – an injury stopped him from becoming a violinist. Served with the Cameronians in the second world war. Known for publications in Scots, books on various aspects of Scotland, and radio and television work.

LI PO (700–762) 80, 224
Chinese poet, a hermit and wanderer who was for a time a court poet. He wrote about many subjects, and was drowned in a drunken effort to embrace the moon.

HENRY WADSWORTH LONGFELLOW (1807–82) 22, 174, 272
American poet, born in Portland, Maine of early New England stock. He travelled extensively in Europe and was a professor at Harvard University.

LLYWELYN LUCAS 139
Australian writer, writing under the pseudonym 'Llywelyn' in the 1960s.

LILIAN BOWES LYON (1855–1949) 105
Related to the Queen Mother, she worked in the Women's Voluntary Service, and lost both her legs in the second world war while she was helping homeless people during the blitz.

THOMAS BABINGTON MACAULAY (1800–59) 92, 276
Educated at Trinity College Cambridge. A politician and a very prestigious historian, he wrote *Lays of Ancient Rome* in 1842.

THOMAS MACDONAGH (1878–1916) 184
Irish patriot and lecturer at the Royal University of Ireland, executed after the Easter Rising.

FINLAY McNAB 245
Described as 'Finlay, the red-haired bard' in *The Book of the Dean of Lismore*, a collection of ancient Gaelic poetry made in the early sixteenth century by Sir James McGregor, Dean of Lismore.

JOHN MASEFIELD (1878–1967) 145, 147, 160, 196
He lived a hard and adventurous life which gave him matter for both verse and prose. It was Chaucer who first inspired him and why, perhaps, he is so successful with long narrative poems. A Poet Laureate, he wrote 'Right Royal' in 1920.

GEORGE MEREDITH (1828–1909) 73
Considered to be one of the great Victorian novelists, he also wrote many fine poems.

W. S. MERWIN (b. 1927) 83
US poet, educated at Princeton University. Lived for a time in Europe. He frequently writes about the natural world.

THOMAS MOORE (1779–1852) 74
Born in Dublin, educated at Trinity College. A poet whose strength was in writing lyrics for songs about Ireland and Irish nationalism. He lived most of his life in Wiltshire.

HARRY MORANT (1864–1902) 29, 43, 172
Born in Britain, he went to Australia in 1883, where his daring horsemanship earned him the title of 'Breaker Morant'. In addition to breaking young horses, he played polo, raced and hunted. He joined up for the South African wars, and in spite of being recommended for leniency for his good service he was shot by firing squad after a court-martial found him guilty of incitement to murder.

WILLIAM MORRIS (1834–96) 209
Poet, artist, decorator, educated at Marlborough and Exeter College Oxford. He worked with Rossetti and Burne-Jones and together they were very influential in English fashion and design.

EDWIN MUIR (1887–1958) 99, 102
Born in the Orkneys and educated at Kirkwall Burgh School until the age of fourteen. First a clerk in a shipbuilding firm, then a freelance journalist, he went to Prague in 1921 and spent the next

seven years travelling the Continent. It was during this period that he became known as a poet, critic and translator.

ALFRED MUNNINGS (1878–1959) 198, 201, 212
Born in Suffolk. His reputation as a horse painter is great, and some of his paintings hang in the Tate Gallery. He was the official artist for the Canadian Government during the first world war. Elected to the Royal Academy in 1919, and became its president in 1944.

LES MURRAY (b. 1938) 95, 98, 110, 261
Grew up on a dairy farm in New South Wales. Described as the most important contemporary Australian poet, and one of the most successful poets writing in the English language today.

DAVID B. NIXON (b. 1925) 104
After many years as a shepherd and farmer, he became a Methodist minister in later life. As well as poetry, he wrote an account of his shepherding years and an opera libretto.

CAROLINE NORTON (1808–77) 37
Granddaughter of the poet and dramatist Richard Brinsley Sheridan, she supported her family by writing. Although she became Lady Stirling-Maxwell shortly before she died, she is invariably known as the Hon. Mrs Norton.

WILL H. OGILVIE (1869–1963) 4, 11, 28, 32, 42, 58, 61, 97, 107, 109, 111, 134, 154, 183, 193, 199, 203, 228, 234, 238, 242, 262
Born in Kelso, Scotland. From 1889 to 1901 he worked in Australia as a drover, horse breaker and bush worker, writing poems and ballads about his experiences. He then settled back in Scotland as a farmer, writer and countryman, though he spent two years lecturing in the USA.

OVID (43 BC–17 AD) 18
Latin poet who died in exile. The *Metamorphoses* is probably his best-known work, and he was translated into English many times from the sixteenth century onwards.

EDWARD PALMER (1885–1959) 240
Interested in poetry since his schooldays in Queensland, Australia. A teacher and writer, he was much influenced by his

experiences in the Australian bush. He lived on and off in Europe where he gained some literary recognition.

A. B. PATERSON (1864–1941) 40, 132
Born New South Wales. Solicitor and war correspondent during the first world war, and also an ambulance driver and remount officer. After the war he was a journalist and editor. He is known for his collection *The Man from Snowy River*.

EDEN PHILLPOTTS (1862–1960) 84
Born in India. Writer of many novels and poems, particularly about Devonshire life, and Dartmoor people and scenery.

ALEXANDER POPE (1688–1744) 151
One of the greatest English poets, well-known for his metrical skills. The child of elderly parents, he was not physically robust. He translated many classical works, including the *Iliad* in about 1717.

BRYAN WALLER PROCTER, pseud. **BARRY CORN-WALL** (1787–1874) 14, 149
Educated at Harrow, he became a solicitor and writer. He was known under his pseudonym as a composer of songs, and under his own name for his plays and biographies.

PENNY RADCLYFFE (b. 1919) 285
Born in Cheshire into a keen hunting family. Breeder of Connemara ponies for thirty years.

THE RIGVEDA 19
A collection of over 1000 Hindu hymns dating from 1500–1000 BC.

RAINER MARIA RILKE (1875–1926) 13
German lyric poet. J. B. Leishman translated his poems into English in 1934.

EDRIC ROBERTS (b. 1891) 33, 115, 117, 122, 131, 135, 187, 192, 195, 202, 233
Captain in the army, he was writing between the wars. A great deal of his poetry was about hunting.

ALAN ROSS (b. 1922) 161
Born in Calcutta, educated at Haileybury and St John's College
Oxford. Served in the Royal Navy during the second world war.

V. SACKVILLE-WEST (1892–1962) 100
Novelist and poet whose writings show her close affiliation with
her country and the land.

SIEGFRIED SASSOON (1886–1967) 156
One of the best of the 'war poets' as well as being a fine prose
writer. His *Memoirs of a Fox-hunting Man* won the Hawthornden
Prize in 1928.

SIR WALTER SCOTT (1771–1832) 45, 169, 275
Born in Edinburgh, the son of a lawyer. Although best known for
his tremendous output of historical novels, he also wrote many fine
poems. While still at school he won praise for his translations of
Virgil and Horace.

WILLIAM SHAKESPEARE (1564–1616) 44, 54, 163, 167,
218, 253, 255, 263
Probably the greatest English playwright and poet.

PERCY BYSSHE SHELLEY (1792–1822) 17, 274
One of the key figures in English romantic poetry. Grandson of a
baronet, he was educated at Eton and University College Oxford.
Married to Mary Shelley, the author of 'Frankenstein'. He was
drowned in a swimming accident off Greece.

SIR PHILIP SIDNEY (1554–86) 216
Said to be one of the best writers of sonnets in England.

G. G. SILL (1791–1859) 82
From one of the early American families in New England.

ROBERT SOUTHEY (1774–1843) 79
Educated at Westminster and Balliol College Oxford, studied law.
Born in Bristol but settled in Keswick, where he wrote poetry and
many books. Poet Laureate.

GLENDA SPOONER 157
Founder of the Ponies of Britain (now Ponies UK) and a highly
qualified judge. Wrote several novels and books on horses.

BETTY STONEHAM 227
Published by *Pony* magazine.

R. S. SURTEES (1803–64) 143
Prolific writer on horses and hunting.

TORQUATO TASSO (1544–95) 248
Significant Italian poet, a contemporary of Edmund Spenser and
a master of the sonnet form.

ALFRED, LORD TENNYSON (1809–1892) 217
A very popular Victorian poet. Fourth son of the Rector of
Somersby, Lincolnshire. Educated at Louth Grammar and Cam-
bridge University.

DYLAN THOMAS (1914–53) 116
Born in Swansea and educated at Swansea Grammar School. He
started life as a journalist, but became something of a legend for
his powerful and sometimes controversial poetry and his lecture
tours. 'Fern Hill' is thought to be one of his most successful poems.

GEORGE WALTER THORNBURY (1828–76) 170
Born in London, his poems caught the mood of English imperial-
ism, but were also inventive and subtle.

TS'EN TS'AN (eighth century) 12
A Chinese official of the T'ang dynasty, he was known as a
distinguished poet.

TU FU (712–770) 41, 47, 70, 121, 128, 136, 237, 241, 246, 250,
260
Chinese lyric poet, much influenced by Li Po. One of China's
greatest poets.

TUDOR ALED (*c.* 1480–1525) 214
Welsh poet, one of the greatest of the period. The bardic tradition
of the Middle Ages reached its climax in his poetry. A gentleman
poet who was a good horseman and athlete.

MARY VAUGHAN (1910–89) 142
Her family came from County Cork in Ireland where her parents
owned a string of racehorses and the local foxhounds. She won a

point-to-point in 1938, riding sidesaddle, and also won the Show Hack Championship at the Royal Show. She lived in Herefordshire.

VOLTAIRE (1694–1778) 190
French writer – poet, dramatist, philosopher etc. He was exiled to England in 1726 and lived there for two or three years.

BILL WALROND (b. 1935) 225
Solicitor, born in Long Melford, Suffolk, and married to Sally Walrond who is well known in the horse driving world. He rode a great deal, including winning a point-to-point, before taking up gliding as a hobby.

R. E. EGERTON WARBURTON (1804–91) 281
Known for his hunting songs and ballads.

VERNON WATKINS (1906–67) 1, 6
Born in Wales of Welsh-speaking parents, a friend of Dylan Thomas. Educated at Repton and Magdalene College Cambridge. Served in the RAF during the second world war.

OLWEN WAY (b. 1923) 152, 205, 232
Born in Pakistan, where her first pony was a Kashmir hill pony. Helped to run her husband Robert's stud, and competed in pony club and show events with her five children. Bred Welsh Cobs and owned and showed Llanarth Cymro, champion under saddle and constant companion for twenty-nine years.

ROBERT WAY (1912–1994) 59
Born in South Africa, he was involved with horses all his life. In the Cavalry OCTU when at Cambridge University, and served in the Mountain Battery during the second world war. At his Newmarket stud he bred several good Thoroughbreds including Flyingbolt. Author of a number of articles on aspects of the horse in history, and several books including *The Garden of the Beloved*.

DOROTHY WELLESLEY (1889–1956) 81, 118
Duchess of Wellington, and a poet admired by Yeats.

JOYCE WEST 239
New Zealand writer of poetry and novels in the 1950s and 1960s.

G. J. WHYTE-MELVILLE (1821–78) 39, 127, 177, 282
Born in Fifeshire. Served in the British army from 1821 to 1849, and in the Crimean war he was an officer in the Turkish Cavalry. Killed in an accident in the hunting field.

WILLIAM WORDSWORTH (1770–1850) 26
One of the great Romantic poets, he was born in Cumberland and spent most of his life there, although he also travelled widely in Europe. He became Poet Laureate in 1843.

XENEPHON (435–354 BC) 254
Born in Athens, he was successful in battle but after siding with the Spartans was exiled. He wrote on many subjects, including cavalry and the well-known *Art of Horsemanship*.

W. B. YEATS (1865–1939) 126, 159, 269
Born in Ireland and educated at schools in Hammersmith and Dublin. He studied art originally, but then turned to literature. With Lady Gregory and others he helped to establish the Irish National Theatre in 1899. Many of his plays and poems had Irish traditionalist and nationalist themes.

NIKOLAI ALEKSEEVICH ZABOLOTSKY (1903–58) 86
Russian poet. He worked in children's publishing, and his first sometimes shocking poems led to a period in exile. His poetry reflects his strong interest in plants and animals.

INDEX OF FIRST
LINES OF POEMS
OR EXTRACTS

~

References are to poem numbers.

A chestnut mare with swerves and heaves   196
A dog starv'd at his Master's Gate   129
A fine little smooth horse colt   7
A horse! A horse! my kingdom for a horse!   54
A hundred mares, all white! their manes   73
A lawn meet: the avenue snaked with its horses   197
A Monk ther was, a fair for the maistrye   181
A painting could not do justice to your red charger   12
After God, we owed the victory to the horses   57
All along the road to the paddock   153
Along the dripping leafless woods   209
Along the mead the hallow'd Steed   79
And all those folk who've had their day   201
And having yoked to her immortal car   17
And horse that, feeding on the grassy hills   221
And I looked, and behold a pale horse   69
And I saw Heaven opened, and behold a white horse   69
And Ruksh, the horse   273
And standing there at her horse's side   198
And the last, my other heart   217
And the talk slid north, and the talk slid south   30
And then, that evening   99
And then to awake, and the farm, like a wanderer white   116
Animals do not sleep. At night   86
Aquiline of matchless speed   248
As I rode home through woods that smelled of evening   207
As May was opening the rosebuds   3

Ask not the Dreamer! See him run   89
At once from Life and from the Chariot driv'n   18
At once the coursers from the barrier bound   148
At the Shows, in full swing   233
'Aye, squire,' said Stevens, 'they back him at evens'   166

Beauty wove for me a woof   232
Before, a dark-haired virgin train   272
Before Gereint, the enemy's punisher   68
Behold   119
Beneath the rainbow silks they sail   61
Beside the dusty road he steps at ease   109
Borysthenes the Alan   283
'Bring forth the horse!' – the horse was brought   243
Brooks too wide for our leaping   256
But for the palfry Gedefer, who stood   277
But he's old – and his eyes are grown hollow   132
But when the Gods were to the forest gone   46
By the snorting chargers   63

Cain as they say with his deep fear disturbed   252
Chucks up his head at the barn's end   113
Come, let me taste my horse   167
Comely and calm, he rides   267
Crisp autumn morning with a pale sun peering   211

Dappled and silver-white   139
Darkness is not dark, nor sunlight the light of the sun   6
Dost thou need a swift grey steed   230

Early and pregnant hour   105
Easy in motion, perfect in his form   146
Eight of the best that ever looked through bridle!   141
Every head across the bar   32
Everyone knows about Duke T'eng's feeling for horses   47

Facing the window, whose red iron rusts   48
Fast, fast, with heels wild spurning   276
Felix Randal, the farrier, O he is dead then?   220
'Fifty – and five – sixty; at sixty'   34
Full many a horse of purest blood, I ween   138
Full tilt for my Emperor and King, I   261

Gael-like is every leap of the dun mare 245
Gaetula harena prosata 284
Gamarra is a noble steed 149
Gentle caress of a muzzle 279
Gipsy gold does not chink and glitter 20
Give me shire-bred team to follow 106
Glen, small, bay horse: since I complained 231
Go strip him, lad! Now, sir, I think you'll declare 39
Going up hill whip me not 52
Grey leaden clouds, slow moving overhead 212

Hacking home in the moonlight, slowly 202
Hail, royal prince! 44
He comes! dread Brama shakes the sunless sky 15
He hasn't got any legs 25
He hears my step at the stable door 124
He lies at rest beneath the shade 280
He never seemed to have a name 195
He stood there, chained to wall and rack 111
He tills the soil today 100
Here where saint and bishop lie in silence 182
Here's to you, Stocking and Star and Blaze! 234
He's not very young and he's not very sound 192
He's sixth – he's fifth – he's fourth – he's third 164
High on the downs the awful ring is made 162
Highway, since you my chief Parnassus be 216
His head! What a beautiful head he's got! 127
His name I have lost in the lapse of the years 262
His sire from the desert, his dam from the north 281
His wall eye stares, white crystal, blue 235
Honour to the coats of red 94
Horses have quick routes they know 200
Horses he loved, and laughter, and the sun 268
Horses, it always seems 88
Horses that stand in the field 137
Horses under 85
How can you know 104
How did he do it? I doubt if he knew it! 188
Hrim-faxi is the sable steed 21

I am not as young as I used to be 131
I am wondering whether to buy you 38

Only the dog's very patient   110
Our young men still may spur the heel   60

Paddy, first owned, was barely fed   235
Pinto is out again! He kicks his door   23
Ponies, ponies for Islington! The patter of eager hoofs   228
Proud English in all things   190
Put the saddle on the mare   186

Round by the black barn and the shrunken pond   108

St George   2
Say'st thou this colt shall prove a swift paced steed   158
See the course throng'd with gazers, the sports are begun   130
She started foaling late at night   285
'*She* was the best that I ever had'   4
Silence wraps the leafless trees   183
Since I have owned an Arab-bred   242
Sired by a hackney (the sire of three Queens)   36
So long, old partner, 'til we meet again   31
So the coward will dare on the gallant horse   257
'So the foemen have fired the gate, men of mine'   173
'Stand, Bayard, stand!' – the steed obeyed   45
Stretched on the Barbary sand you lie   284
Surely hunting is cruel?   189

That big timber took some dodging, but our hacks were tried
   and true   29
The eldest son bestrides him   270
The eye can hardly pick them out   120
The glory of his nostrils is terrible   55
The hammer has fallen, the auctioneer nods   33
The Heavenly Horse has come from the caves of Yueh-shih   80
The horses skidded on the black-iced road   204
The horses stand on stormy skies   118
The huntsman's horse, whether brown or bay   187
The immortal Sun   17
The mare lies down in the grass where the nest of the skylark is
   hidden   1
The mark of a stake in the shoulder   134
The old brown horse looks over the fence   123
The Protector-General of Anhsi has a dark barbarian piebald   237

PUBLISHER'S ACKNOWLEDGEMENTS

~

The publishers wish to acknowledge the sources and thank the following for permission to use the poems and extracts reproduced in this collection.

'Hunter Trials' by John Betjeman from *Collected Poems*, by permission of John Murray (Publishers) Ltd.

'Breaking Out', 'Cheltenham Races', 'Five Horses', 'Homecoming', 'Horse Dealing', 'Snowbound' and 'Welsh Song' by Alison Brackenbury from *Breaking Ground*, by permission of the author and Carcanet Press Limited, and 'After the X-Ray', first published in *The Spectator*.

'Brooks too wide for our leaping' by Pam Brown from *Horse Quotations*, edited by Helen Exley, reprinted with permission of Exley Publications Ltd.

'The Stockman' by David Campbell from *Speak with the Sun* published by Chatto & Windus, by permission of Random House UK Ltd.

'Horses on the Camargue' by Roy Campbell, by permission of Francisco Campbell Custodio and Ad. Donker (Pty) Ltd.

'Cambridgeshire' by Frances Cornford, by permission of the Trustees of Mrs F. C. Cornford.

'Dodgers Leap' by Dalesman, by permission of the editor, *Horse and Hound*.

'Dreams' by Walter de la Mare, by permission of the Literary Trustees of Walter de la Mare, and The Society of Authors as their literary representative.

'The Horse' by Ronald Duncan, published by Alan Tabar Ltd, by permission of David Higham Associates.

'I must sell my horse' from *Silver, Sand and Snow* by Eleanor Farjeon, published by Michael Joseph, by permission of David Higham Associates.

'The Runaway' and 'Stopping by Woods on a Snowy Evening' by Robert Frost, published by Jonathan Cape, by permission of Random House UK Limited.

Extract from *Venus Observed* (1950) by Christopher Fry, by permission of Oxford University Press.

'The Cantering Foal' by George Rostrevor Hamilton from *Collected Poems*, by permission of William Heinemann Ltd.

'When first a mother bore you' by Patrick Hore Ruthven from *Joy of Youth*, by permission of Peter Davies Ltd.

'The Ploughman' by Wilfred Howe-Nurse, by permission of Basil Blackwell Ltd.

'A Dream of Horses' by Ted Hughes, by permission of Faber & Faber Ltd.

'Birth of the Foal' by Ferenc Juhász, translated from the Hungarian by David Wevill, published by Penguin Books.

Extract from *The Time Piece* by Frank Kendon, by permission of Cambridge University Press.

'The Fall of Leaf' by Maurice Lindsay from *Snow Warning*, by permission of the Linden Press.

'Right Royal', 'The Racer', 'An Epilogue' and 'Reynard the Fox' by John Masefield, by permission of The Society of Authors as the literary representative of the Estate of John Masefield.

Extract from *Green with Beasts* by W. S. Merwin, published by Harper Collins, reprinted by permission of David Higham Associates.

'The Horses' and 'Horses' by Edwin Muir, by permission of Faber & Faber Ltd.

'The Assimilation of Background', 'The Barrenjoey', 'The Lieutenant of Horse Artillery' and 'The Tube' by Les Murray from *Collected Poems*, by permission of Carcanet Press Limited.

'Tribute Due' by David B. Nixon, with permission of Anna Nixon and thanks to Edward Hart.

'The Old Mare's Foal', 'The Battered Brigade', 'Between the Woods', 'Storm-Stayed', 'The Arab Test' from *Scattered Scarlet*; 'A Comrade', 'The Remount Train', 'The Waler', 'The

~ 328 ~

Horseman', 'The Stallion', 'Banshee', 'Hacking Home', 'To You' from *Galloping Shoes*; 'The Gymkhana King' from *Saddles Again*; 'Polo Ponies' and 'The Master Horseman' from *Over the Grass*; 'Clydesdales', 'The Steeplechasers', 'Lanyard', 'Ponies for Islington', 'Bridle Hand' from *A Handful of Leather*, all by Will H. Ogilvie and published by Constable, by permission of George T. A. Ogilvie.

'The Carthorses' by E. Phillpotts, by kind permission of Gerald Duckworth & Co. Ltd.

'The Boy' by R. M. Rilke, from *Selected Poems*, translated by J. B. Leishman and published by J. B. Woolf, by permission of Random House UK Ltd.

'Four-Year-Old', 'Stable Memories', 'Out at Grass', 'Pensioned', 'The Old 'Un', 'The Hireling', 'The Huntsman's Horse', 'Seabird', 'The Liver-Coloured Chestnut', 'Blessings' and 'Kildare' by Edric Roberts, published in *The Field*, and *Somewhere in England* and *Winter Magic* published by Constable.

'The Land' © 1927 by Vita Sackville-West, reproduced by permission of Curtis Brown London on behalf of the Estate of Vita Sackville-West.

'What the Captain said at the Point-to-Point' by Siegfried Sassoon, by permission of George Sassoon.

'Fern Hill' by Dylan Thomas from *The Poems* published by J. M. Dent, by permission of David Higham Associates.

'Red Rum' by Mary Vaughan from *Great Horses and Gallant Horseman* published by Quiller Press, by permission of Oliver Vaughan.

'The Mare' from *Cypress and Acacia* (1959) and 'Foal' from *The Lady with the Unicorn* (1948) by Vernon Watkins, published by Faber & Faber Ltd, by permission of Gwen Watkins.

'The Face of the Horse' by N. A. Zablotsky, from *Scrolls: Selected Poems by N. A. Zablotsky*, published by Jonathan Cape, by permission of Random House UK Ltd.